Understanding, Expounding and Obeying God's Word

Understanding, Expounding and Obeying God's Word

Methods and advice to help you study and apply the Bible

Alan Stibbs

Authentic

MILTON KEYNES ● COLORADO SPRINGS ● HYDERABAD

Understanding God's World First published 1950 by Inter-Varsity Fellowship
Expounding God's Word – First published 1960 by Inter-Varsity Press
Obeying God's Word – First published 1955 by Inter-Varsity Press

15 14 13 12 11 10 09   7 6 5 4 3 2 1

This edition first published 2009 by Authentic Media
9 Holdom Avenue, Bletchley, Milton Keynes, Bucks, MK1 1QR, UK
1820 Jet Stream Drive, Colorado Springs, CO 80921, USA
OM Authentic Media, Medchal Road, Jeedimetla Village, Secunderabad 500 055, A.P., India
www.authenticmedia.co.uk
Authentic Media is a division of IBS-STL U.K., limited by guarantee, with its Registered Office at Kingstown Broadway, Carlisle, Cumbria CA3 0HA. Registered in England & Wales No. 1216232. Registered charity 270162

British Library Cataloguing in Publication Data
A catalogue record for this book is available from the
British Library
ISBN-13: 978-1-85078-843-0

Cover design by Don Collins
Print Management by Adare
Printed and bound in the UK by J. F. Print Ltd., Sparkford, Somerset

Understanding God's Word

Contents

Preface

The simple purpose of this book is to suggest to willing seekers and would-be students of divinely-revealed truth ways in which they may pursue more fully and with increased understanding the study, faith and practice of God's written Word. Much briefer summaries of the same material have already been made available in some of my other books. It is hoped that this fresh, independent publication of a greatly expanded treatment of the same general theme may be used to reach a wider circle of new readers, and that it may help them and those who may have read the brief articles referred to above to a deeper appreciation and a more effective practical application of the principles both of biblical interpretation and obedience. Readers who are likely to be encouraged to study the apparently more theoretical sections by first seeing the practical relevance of the general theme to actual Christian living are advised to read Chapter 6 at the beginning as well as at the end of their study of this book.

May God increase proper understanding and helpful use of His Word in all ways and by all means; and may the reading of this book lead some to a new or better use of such ways and means.

Alan Stibbs

1

Introduction

> All Scripture is God-breathed and is useful for teaching, rebuking, correcting and training in righteousness, so that the man of God may be thoroughly equipped for every good work. (2 Tim. 3:16,17)

This is written to help those who believe that we have in Holy Scripture a Book of authoritative, God-given revelation and instruction to which we must turn to know the truth, and from which we are meant to learn, first, what God has done in Christ for our redemption, and, second, how we are to live lives that will please God. As Christians the Bible is our one standard textbook, our rule of faith, our final court of appeal. It is a treasure committed to us, of which we are the stewards. It is our responsibility to use it rightly by reverent approach, accurate understanding, obedient response, and diligent propagation.

Granted that one has this reverent approach to the Bible – the humble believing recognition of its divine inspiration – the next thing of supreme importance is its right understanding. We cannot be truly sound in the faith unless we let it inform all our beliefs; nor can we arrive at correct convictions unless we first set ourselves to understand exactly what it does teach. This goal of true understanding is not one easily reached. Its pursuit requires prayerful diligence, painstaking labour, and sustained quest. If I have not as yet grasped the true meaning of the Word of God, I cannot as yet either properly obey it or intelligently proclaim it. If I aim to stand before others, glorying in the Bible as the Book of God-given revelation, and professing to be its expositor, surely I ought first to take care to see that what I am going to say is a faithful and justifiable interpretation of Scripture and not merely some hanging of my own conjecture on a Scripture peg?

The experience of humble believers is that, whatever their intellectual limitations, God rewards diligent seekers, and speaks to their souls through His Word. But it is never right to rest satisfied with our inevitably limited knowledge. We are all called to undertake some of that labour which is the condition of understanding more. For it is true of Scripture, as of God's gifts in general, that it corresponds to our powers of appreciation and response. While the gift is all of God, we have to become active, and to sustain our activity, if we are fully to possess its benefits. The same is true of the harvest of the field. There are laws of fruitfulness which the farmer must observe. At every stage in the whole process of preparation, growth, and ingathering there are specific tasks which the farmer must do. If he fails at any one point, the advancing process will be hindered, and the ultimate harvest impaired. Similarly, if our lives and our service, as those called to obey and proclaim the revealed Word of God, are to yield their full harvest to God's glory, there is work to be done. Before we can properly serve the Word of God we must properly understand it. Otherwise, there is a serious danger lest in our excess of enthusiasm we actually misrepresent it.

If the Bible is 'the most valuable thing which this world affords', it is surely wrong to use it carelessly and casually, to presume to know what it teaches without first taking great pains to discover exactly what it does teach. Because we all have our prejudices and misconceptions, it is all too easy to see in the Bible only what we want to see, and to miss the new and edifying revelation of fuller truth which is God's purpose for us, but which depends upon our using His Word rightly. What is even worse, it is all too easy to read our own ideas into the Bible instead of getting out of the Bible what it teaches, which might quite possibly overthrow our ideas. Such handling of the Word of God is a presumptuous imposition of personal prejudice rather than a humble exposition of God-given revelation.

There is, therefore, much need for us all to be 'disciples' before we become 'apostles'. We need to spend much time as learners in God's school if we are to do God's will in the world and to stand before men and women as true ministers of the gospel. In other words, that true understanding of Scripture, which is absolutely essential to its right and worthy use, cannot be gained just by offering a prayer before we read. We must also be prepared to take time and trouble, to become students, to use our God-given powers of intelligence and judgment.

The purpose of this book is to give some elementary guidance and practical suggestions to those who are prepared to become workers in the school of biblical understanding. Let's remember that the Apostle Paul wrote to Timothy: 'Do your best to present yourself to God as one approved, a workman who does not need to be ashamed and who correctly handles the word of truth' (2 Tim. 2:15).

2

Getting at the True Text

Attempted definitions of the inspiration of the Bible sometimes include the statement that the words were inspired 'as originally given'. This is but another way of recognizing that before the message of Scripture has reached us the original writing has had to be both copied and translated. This introduces at least the possibility that in these processes some of the full value of the original may have been lost.

Here we can at once recognize with gratitude God's amazing providence in connection with His Word written. The text of Holy Scripture is far and away much better preserved than that of any other ancient writings. Also the very language of the original is of such a character that it is much more capable of being translated than many works of great authors. This is the more true because the Bible is not a book of abstract definitions, but chiefly a book of examples – a book of concrete history. In addition, its idioms and metaphors are so taken from the common life of humanity and are so vivid and lifelike that they can be successfully transplanted and readily take root and flourish in completely new soil. What is more, some translations, of which the King James Version is the outstanding example, can themselves be said to be 'inspired', and have become recognized as literary classics in the language of their adoption. For God caused them to be translated at a formative time and they themselves have become formative through the influence which they have had on the thought and speech of the people.

It is evident that since biblical Hebrew and New Testament Greek are no longer in current use, and are unknown to the majority, even of Christians, translations are indispensable; and so all attempts faithfully to express the meaning of the original may have their value. According to their merits, all fresh and different translations, together with paraphrases and commentaries, should be welcomed and used. For instance, the would-be student of the Word of God should not read only the one. He ought also to refer to other translations in order to increase his understanding of the true meaning of the original.

Such fresh renderings of the original text can, of course, be of full value only if those who have made them have put into them the labour and skill of much study, research and scholarly judgment. Here at once is a sphere in which, if we would know what the Scriptures actually teach, we are dependent upon the painstaking work of scholars – otherwise we could not read the Bible in our own language at all. Here is one reason why we should be prepared ourselves to take pains to increase our understanding of the exact and full meaning of what was originally written. If scholarship and much specialized study are essential, as they are, to the discovery and exposition of all the treasures of the Bible, those who believe the Bible to be the very oracle of God ought to be the most energetic at giving themselves to this kind of labour.

All translations, even the best, still have their limitations. It is often quite impossible for a translator to find words adequately to express some fine shade of meaning in the original. One must be content with conveying the general sense, or a mere suggestion of the meaning. The same word in the original may in different contexts have to be rendered by different words in English or, alternatively, different words in the original may be rendered by the same word in English. This means that suggestions in the original either of similarity or difference are lost or even contradicted in the process of translation. This is not the translators' fault. They can only do their best with the words at their disposal. But, as those who ought to know and to be able to expound exactly what the Bible teaches, we surely shall be at fault if, with opportunities at hand waiting to be used, we make no attempt to get beyond the limitations of translations to a truer and more exact appreciation of the meaning of the original.

The great need, therefore, is to get at the original text and its true meaning. So all aids should be used that in any way bring us nearer to this goal. Best of all, of course, is a direct personal acquaintance with the original languages; and it is surprising what can be accomplished in this direction by those whose heart is in the task. Where there is a will there is a way. Also, as a good second best, where it is impossible to become expert in the original languages themselves, it is possible to go half-way and get that much nearer to a more accurate understanding by the use of many aids specially prepared to help such limited study. For instance, an analytical concordance with anglicized renderings of the originals does at least enable one to recognize when the same or different words are used in the original, and what is the more particular meaning of the words which are used.

Finally, in this connection, if we are to get as near as possible to the exact wording of the original, there is a place for the work of textual critics. These must be specialists who not only know the original languages, but who have acquired skill and discernment in the reading and comparison of ancient manuscripts. Such criticism is, of course, constructive not destructive. Its object is to recover as far as possible the original text. This involves the careful identification and close examination of variant readings, and also the detection of obvious corruptions and possible later emendations due to slips in transcription or to a scribe's desire to 'improve' the text by simplifying a difficulty or trying to correct a previous scribe's mistake. It may involve as well choosing between outstanding alternatives, both possibly of early origins, or, in very rare cases, the suggestion of a possible emendation or more likely reading.

Manuscripts tend to fall into groups. Those which share many of the same features and variants in their text presumably had a common origin. They bear witness together to one comparatively early form of the text. After manuscripts have been thus classified or grouped, the different early variations of reading which each group represents still have to be compared. In choosing between them it is a generally accepted canon of criticism to prefer the more difficult reading, simply because it is more likely that a scribe altered a passage to make it less difficult than that one altered it to make it more so. The choice between alternative readings may become very occasionally more than a matter of mere textual criticism. It may need the judgment of the New Testament historian and theologian, who has grounds other than those of the immediate manuscript evidence for having a preference. A remarkable fact about the preservation of the text, however, is that no doctrine is threatened by textual uncertainties.

These discrepancies between manuscripts have served a most beneficial purpose. They have awakened and stimulated intellectual inquiry and investigation, leading to positive results of great value. We are now more sure of the text of the original Bible than our ancestors were. We know how amazingly well the text of Scripture has been preserved. As Christians we have every right to say that our documentary evidence is so outstandingly good that it is in a class by itself. The margin of possible error is virtually negligible.

What seems surprising and regrettable is that in recent years those who have held most strongly to orthodox faith in the Bible as the inspired Word of God have largely left this work of investigating the details of the treasure of revelation to those whose attitude has been more liberal and rationalistic. Is it not time that we confessed to our shame our shortcomings in this direction and did something to take possession of a field of study which ought to be peculiarly our own? For if any people ought to be prepared to sweat and toil, to take endless pains, in order to ascertain first what Scripture says and second what it means, it ought to be those who accept it as God's Word written for our learning. It is high time that we had within our own ranks a real revival of first-class biblical scholarship. This is the more desirable because many missionary and unevangelized fields still wait for the revision, completion or first translation in their languages of the Word of God. This can be done well only with consecrated scholarship.

3

Understanding the Text

Once you have before you the biblical text the next requisite is rightly to understand the sense so as to be able both to grasp and to give the meaning. In order properly to achieve this end several things are desirable. These may be indicated in the form of general rules or guiding lines of procedure.

(i) *Get at the true meaning of single words*. Here detailed exactness is of supreme importance. This is a study whose demands are most exacting and whose possibilities are inexhaustible. For the sense of Scripture is determined by the words. Therefore every single word matters. And this consideration, true in any case, becomes much more important if we believe that the divine inspiration extended to the words and secured the selecting of particularly appropriate ones. Here are some practical hints.

(a) Words are to be taken in their common or usual meaning (unless such meaning can be shown from the context or from the general witness of Scripture to be inappropriate). If we are to use words intelligibly and not arbitrarily their sense must be fixed by usage.

(b) An increased understanding of the sense of particular words should be acquired from a study of their actual use and the comparison of their different occurrences.

(c) Words are to be taken in the sense in which they would have been understood by their original hearers or readers. This rule particularly applies, of course, to words which may subsequently have acquired a secondary or developed sense. This same rule also applies to the use of old translations like the King James Version: e.g. 'prevent' means to 'anticipate' or 'precede' in Ps. 119:147 and 1 Thes. 4:15; 'let' means to 'hinder' or 'restrain' in Isa. 43:13 and 2 Thes. 2:7.

(d) Words sometimes change their meaning completely with the passage of time.

(e) Some words acquire a special meaning in the Bible from biblical usage alone and in consequence of the progress and enlargement of the content of revelation. Study, for example, the phrase 'the Lord's anointed'. See 1 Sam. 24:10; Ps. 2:2; Acts 4:26; Rev. 11:15.

(ii) *Get at the use, syntax and idiom of the original language.* We need to grasp the significance of difference in usage, the form in which sentences are constructed, the method of the expression of ideas. The following 'rules' may help.

(a) Be careful to punctuate and to read correctly. For example, in John 12:27 by substituting a question mark for a colon after the words 'Father, save me from this hour' in the NIV rendering, the sense is made much more clear.

(b) Note whether a statement is indicative, interrogative or imperative, definite or conditional, actual or hypothetical, etc. See the difference between the NIV and KJV in John 5:39 and Rom. 5:1.

(c) In Greek note the force of tenses, prepositions, the definite article, the emphatic personal pronoun, etc. A few examples will underline the importance of this. 1 Cor. 3:6: 'I have planted [aorist – one act], Apollos watered [aorist]; but God was all the time giving the increase [imperfect – continuous action]' (KJV). Heb. 12:2: 'Looking – away from all else – unto Jesus' (KJV). Here the verb in Greek whose participle is translated 'looking' is a compound form with a preposition meaning 'away from' in front of the main root meaning 'to see'. The name of the Holy Spirit in Greek requires the article when He is spoken of personally, but when the reference is to His work, manifestation and gift to humankind, the article is almost invariably omitted. See John 16:13 and 20:22, etc. Note the meaning of Matt. 5:18: I [emphatic] tell you the truth,' and Matt. 28:5: 'Do not be afraid' (i.e. like the soldiers on guard have done – see verse 4).

(d) Note that Hebrew ways of thinking and speaking are often very different from ours. Ideas which we may have been accustomed to attach to certain words of the Bible may need revising in the light of Hebrew usage. For example, the phrase 'I have loved Jacob, but Esau I have hated' (Mal. 1:2,3), is the Hebrew way of stating not so much a direct opposite as a comparison; viz: 'I loved Jacob more than Esau.' Such a way of putting it means that in Hebrew idiom there are no 'greys'; everything is either 'black' or 'white'. For a New Testament parallel showing how Hebrew idiom may underlie New Testament expressions compare Luke 14:26 and Matt. 10:37.

(e) Note that the more purely Greek idiom needs to be understood by comparison with the spoken Greek current in the first century AD rather than with classical Greek. This is a field of study which is giving fresh treasures to the careful seeker. For instance, it now appears that when it says in Luke 15:13 that 'the younger son got together all he had' it means that he 'realized his estate' and turned it into ready money.

Under this general heading of idiom and usage there is an endless field for research and illuminating discovery. These examples touch only the fringe of the subject.

(iii) *Get at the form of expression*. It is most important to know whether a particular passage is literal or figurative, actual or metaphorical. Figurative terms should be interpreted accordingly. Note should be taken both of the force and of the limitations of special forms of expression such as dramatic personification, the use of anthropomorphic and anthropopathic language in reference to God, and the language of 'appearance' – which describes things as we see them, e.g. the rising and setting of the sun.

(iv) *Get at the character of the composition*. The passage to be studied may be fact or fiction, history or allegory, prose or poetry, narrative or discourse, soliloquy or dialogue, etc. For example, some of the psalms are responsive (see 15 and 24). In Romans 3 there is a virtual dialogue between Paul and an imaginary objector. Psalm 22:1 and the following verses represent a sufferer as in dying agonies able to articulate only a few disjointed words at a time. It is, therefore, out of place to supply words and so make every sentence complete. Rather translate literally its broken phrases: 'My God! my God!

Why have you forsaken me? Far from saving me! Words of my groaning!' In Ps. 109 some maintain that 'saying' should be supplied at the end of verse 6, and the imprecations of verses 6 to 19 read as those of the psalmist's enemies. Then verse 20 must be read, 'This is my adversaries' award to me, and this is the sentence that they would procure against me from the Lord.'

(v) *Aim to appreciate the allusions, figures, and expressions* which are related to the customs, circumstances, etc., of the original readers. For instance, contrast Isa. 3:13, 'The LORD takes his place in court;' and Joel 3:12, 'There I will sit to judge all the nations on every side.' Such language is drawn from the habits of Oriental courts, where advocates stand up to plead and judges sit down to pronounce sentence.

(vi) *Recognize literary customs* prevalent at the time of writing, particularly if different from our own.

   (a) Hebrew literary methods and motives were different from those to which we are accustomed. Interest in history as history was virtually unknown. The aim was to improve the reader's mind. The record is called 'prophecy'; it is a moral evaluation.
   (b) The incorporation of whole sections from other writers verbatim without specific acknowledgment was not regarded as improper plagiarism.
   (c) Duplicate narratives. Two different accounts of the same events may be put alongside each other without any attempt at reconciliation or combination. This is left to the reader. Like the parallelism of Hebrew poetry, the two expressions are not reduced into one composite picture by the author, but are left to stand side by side, so that the reader can get more from the two together than from one alone.

(d) Paul's epistles have features common to the letter-writing of his day. For example, he dictated most of his letters to an amanuensis, and added only a salutation or a personal postscript in his own handwriting.

(vii) *Do not be misled by chapter or other divisions*, or by added chapter headings, etc., which are no part of the original, and may be inappropriate, 1 Cor. 11:1 for instance, should be connected with what precedes; Eph. 1:15 to 2:7 forms a connected whole. This means, to state the point positively, that connecting links should be recognized. For example, sentences which include a 'therefore' (like Rom. 5:1, 8:1, 12:1; Heb. 4:1, 6:1 and 12:1) must be understood in the light of what has gone before.

(viii) *Try to understand the particular significance of each separate passage*. This is a very important rule. For true understanding of the text of Scripture it is necessary to appreciate the circumstances of composition and the immediate point of particular references. One needs to enter into the writer's environment and outlook, his reaction to prevailing conditions, and his conscious purpose in writing. This involves an acquaintance with the background and historical setting. One ought to read the Old Testament historical books to get a better understanding of the order and importance of the prophets; and read Acts in order to place and fully to appreciate some of the letters of Paul. Also, Paul's epistles deal with particular conditions, problems, and errors prevailing at that time in particular churches. His letters cannot be properly understood and their lasting lessons properly appreciated unless these features are first studied. Attention should therefore be given first to the original and literal sense.

(ix) *Beware of introducing conceptions foreign to the original text* that is, allowing words to suggest ideas not intended by the writer. Fancy easily runs riot, and one tends to see in the Bible not what is really there, but only a reflection of one's own ideas. The sixteenth-century Protestant Reformers were particularly alive to the seriousness of this danger. Wycliffe warned against reading into the Bible what the Spirit does not mean. The later Reformers put emphasis on the literal sense of the Bible because they were very conscious that current ecclesiastical interpretations were artificial and a virtual rejection of the Word of God.

(x) *Recognize the character of divine revelation as given in and through history.* God has spoken not by words only but in and through the lives of people, and most of all in and through the life, death and resurrection of His Son incarnate. God primarily reveals Himself by His doings, and inspires His prophets to interpret these doings to all. See Amos 3:7. Therefore the words of the prophets are complementary to the deeds or events that they interpret. They provide the interpretation of the revelation given in the history. In this way events have a tongue. They speak; or rather God speaks in them. The outstanding events of this historical and biblical revelation are the call of Abraham, the deliverance of the Israelites from Egypt, and the revelation to Moses at Sinai and to the long line of prophets in the preparatory dispensation. Later we have the calling of disciples to follow Jesus, the ministry, death and resurrection of our Lord, the Pentecostal gift of the Spirit, His manifold working in the church and that inspiration of the apostles which produced the New Testament writings in the final Christian dispensation. To the Christian, therefore, and to the believer in divine revelation, these historical events matter supremely. Christianity is a historic revelation. God has been revealed in flesh and blood and by events in time and space. As the Apostles' Creed expresses it, our Lord 'suffered under Pontius Pilate'. Therefore, the original, literal, historical meaning of Scripture is of fundamental importance.

(xi) Recognize the character of what is revealed in the Bible, namely, spiritual truth otherwise unknown. The prophets were inspired to see and to express things new, things which to the finite mind are unfathomable and inexpressible, things for which men have no current vocabulary. There were two inevitable consequences.

(a) The use of analogy or figure. The new and hitherto unknown can be suggested or described only by comparison with the known. So Scripture is full of what are expressly called in one place 'a copy of the true one' (Heb. 9:24). The heavenly realm, for instance, is always described in this obviously figurative way.

(b) The use of current words in a new biblical sense. Because no adequate descriptive terms existed in the language, the prophets of God had often to take existing words and fill them by their use of them with a new meaning. This is what the Bible continues to do when it is translated into other languages. It tends sooner or later, as its influence increases, to give to common and generic words a unique and specific Christian meaning. So the very word 'god' comes to be written 'God', and to mean the one and only, the living and true God. See 1 Cor. 8:3–6.

This means, therefore, that in the understanding of the words of the Bible one should be guided finally by biblical usage. To the true reader many words ultimately mean what they have come to mean by their use in Scripture. So words like 'love' (*agape*) and 'humility' (*tapeinophrosune*) and 'godliness' (*eusebeia*) mean to the New Testament scholar something very different from what they mean in classical Greek. There is, indeed, a language of Zion, a language of the People of God. Truly progressive students of the Bible cannot but become expert in it. But it has to be learnt by study and discriminating use, like any other language; and what is more, none can truly understand it except the redeemed.

4

Interpreting the Text: General Rules

The Christian's use of the Bible does not end when you have succeeded in understanding the text; rather, the more direct Christian use can now begin. For it has an abiding practical purpose. These things written long ago were written for our edification and admonition. The Bible is meant to be a spiritual guidebook, a chart of the seas of life, to show us the right way, to make us wise to salvation, to enable us to know the truth by which we can be set free and sanctified (see Rom. 15:4; 1 Cor. 10:11; 2 Tim. 3:15–17; John 8:31,32, 17:17). If it is to serve this more immediate practical end it must be interpreted rightly. We need to be able not only to give the original sense but also to discern the larger and abiding significance. Let us now seek, therefore, to make ourselves aware of some general rules of interpretation.

(i) *Interpret grammatically*. Words must be taken in their proper sense. There is no justification for letting the words mean something to us which they could never have meant in the original language, and may not even mean in the translation before us.

(ii) *Interpret in relation to the context*. The meaning of a word or phrase is often modified by the connection in which it is used. One must let its setting determine its particular sense and significance. For the context often clearly limits the meaning of a word or statement and prevents it from being taken in more than one sense. This rule particularly applies to words which have more than one meaning, and to phrases or statements which are ambiguous, or can suggest an entirely different idea if taken by themselves out of their context.

(a) Note, for instance, the very different meanings of the same word 'faith' in the following four contexts: Gal. 1:23, 'the man . . . is now preaching the faith he once tried to destroy'; Rom. 3:3, 'Shall their unbelief make the faith [faithfulness, NIV] of God without effect?' (KJV); 2 Cor. 5:7, 'We live by faith, not by sight'; Acts 14:27, God 'had opened the door of faith to the Gentiles'.

(b) In Josh. 24:15 the words 'choose for yourselves this day whom you will serve' refer not, as often suggested, to the choice between serving the Lord or serving other gods, but to the choice between different false gods which those must make who will not serve the Lord.

(c) In John 9:3 the words 'Neither this man nor his parents sinned' are not to be taken out of their context as a declaration of absolute sinlessness. Their meaning is strictly limited by the question in verse 2 to which they are an answer. They mean that the man's blindness was not caused by his own sin or his parents' sin.

(d) Words from Jas. 5:14,15 cannot be quoted to support the Roman doctrine of extreme unction for the salvation of the soul of the dying, because the context makes plain that the kind of salvation here referred to is physical, i.e. restoration to health.

(iii) *Have regard to the character and purpose of the whole book or larger section*. This is sometimes expressly mentioned, viz: Luke 1:1–4; John 20:31. But often it can be appreciated only by study. It is most important, therefore, not just to read and quote odd texts in isolation, but to get familiar with them not only in their immediate setting but also in their larger context. The benefit of our study is greatly increased when we read sections and books as a whole, not solely in disconnected fragments. Also we ought to take trouble to find out everything we can about the circumstantial setting and immediate occasion of the writing, so as to be able to appreciate the purpose of the writer. This particularly applies, for instance, to the writings of the prophets and to most of Paul's epistles; for example, Amos and Galatians. This is why the section in commentaries generally known as 'Introduction' ought to be read.

(a) Psalms 120 – 134, 'the Songs of Degrees', were written to be used by the pilgrims on their way up to Jerusalem to the great festivals. The significance of some of the verses can be appreciated only when this is recognized.

(b) A comparison of 1 Cor. 1:12 and 3:22 shows that in the latter verse Paul still has the same subject in mind, viz: ministers belong to the Christians, not the Christians to their ministers. Compare 4:1. Obviously, therefore, if one is to appreciate the full significance of 3:22 one must see it in its place in the larger whole, i.e. in the section 1:10 – 4:17 in which Paul deals with ministers, their message and their ministry.

(c) Rom. 3:28 and Jas. 2:24 are sometimes quoted as contradictory. A study of the two epistles shows that the larger purpose of the writer was different in each case. While Paul is attacking works which claim to take the place of faith as the ground of salvation, James is protesting against that kind of empty profession of faith, or 'barren orthodoxy', which does not express response to God in active obedience, and therefore is not the faith which saves. Compare Rom. 4:1–5 and Jas. 2:21–23.

(iv) *Recognize the divine inspiration of the Bible.* This means, in other words, acknowledge in these writings the purpose of God as well as the purpose of the human writer. This divine purpose may be much greater and more far-reaching than any purpose which could have been consciously or intelligibly present to the actual writers.

(a) Some of the prophets were aware that the divine Spirit of prophecy in them was bearing witness to things yet to come, the full significance or ultimate fulfilment of which they could not grasp. See 1 Pet. 1:10–12. But our position is different. We live in the light of New Testament fulfilment. Therefore, we may rightly expect to appreciate and to use parts of the Old Testament in a way in which people could not do before Christ came.

(b) Paul wrote his letters to particular churches and individuals with reference to their immediate circumstances. He could scarcely have been aware that his writings were to become the authoritative Scriptures of the church throughout the centuries. Therefore we may rightly see in some of the things included in these writings a higher purpose and a larger providence than any of which Paul can have been conscious. Christian faith recognizes in these writings not only an immediate objective of the human writer, but also an abiding age-long purpose of the inspiring

Spirit. Such writings must be reverenced and interpreted in the light and under the constraint of this bigger conviction.

(c) A remarkable illustration of this principle is provided in the one utterance of Caiaphas which is regarded as prophecy. See John 11:47–53. Here Caiaphas had his own obvious meaning and purpose. He spoke as a scheming politician. His counsel was one of expediency. He argued that it was better that the potential leader of a Messianic rising against the Romans should be put to death rather than that a condition of things should be allowed to develop which might involve the whole Jewish people in fresh overthrow by the Romans. But his words are regarded as prophecy by the writer of the gospel record, because they are capable of a second and much more significant meaning. For Caiaphas was the high priest. It was his responsibility once a year to offer the atoning sacrifice for the nation. And in this year, the year in which all types were fulfilled, he himself proposed that, so to speak, not an animal victim but a man should die for the nation, and that man Jesus of Nazareth. In other words, though he knew it not, he fulfilled his high priestly office and pointed out Jesus as 'the Lamb of God', who by His death should make propitiation for the sins of the people and thus save them from danger. This deeper meaning was clearly the one which the Spirit who inspired the words, purposed to express.

(v) *Distinguish inspiration of record from direct and dogmatic utterances of God and of God's messengers.* There are many words in the Bible which are clearly not the direct words of God. Yet they are words which He has caused to be written because they record things from which we can profit, and the record is so inspired as to bring out the points of most significance. Parts of the Old Testament which we should call history, such as Joshua, Judges, 1 and 2 Samuel, 1 and 2 Kings, the Jews called 'prophecy': they regarded them as records of events written up by men with spiritual insight, and therefore of value for spiritual edification. On this point A.T. Pierson wrote

> When Satan says, 'You will not die', when Job and his three friends discuss the problem and philosophy of evil; when the blind man, whose eyes were opened by Christ, argues with the Pharisees; when, in a word, the Bible narrates human events or records human utterances in which God is not represented either as acting or speaking through man, inspiration covers only the essential accuracy of the narrative. But when God directs a course to be pursued, or Himself guides an utterance, the sanction of His infallible authority is thus given. (*Stumbling Stones Removed*, p. 42)

(vi) *Beware equally of a limiting literalism and of a fanciful or an evasive spiritualization.* There is always danger in one-sided extremes in the interpretation of Scripture. We need to learn to keep the balance between the extremes; to be prepared, as we use Scripture, to see heavenly visions on the mountain-top and yet always to be willing to return at once to the waiting valley of earthly reality. Excessive literalism exhausts and limits the meaning of Scripture. It is not enough to hold solely to the letter of the law. It is the spirit that quickens. Because the concrete details of the Bible illustrate and express general principles, those who would learn from its statements must be prepared to see their wider spiritual application. There are, for instance, principles of Christian conduct enunciated in 1 Corinthians 8 which apply to many more problems than the particular one which Paul was facing when he wrote that chapter. On the other hand, excessive spiritualization turns the liberty of the Spirit into licence. It often permits the interpreter to avoid the plain moral teaching of the passage and to read into it imaginative and possibly unpractical and rather useless theories of his own. The concrete detail of Scripture has its lasting significance, encouraging us to follow present duty rather than indulge in worthless speculation.

(vii) *Recognize the main purpose of all the Bible, namely to reveal the ways of God* with us and for all people, particularly sinful people. Only those who recognize this can use Scripture rightly. For it makes certain fundamental assumptions, and is addressed to a particular need and end. It assumes that we are God's creatures, meant to find life in fellowship with Him, and yet living in revolt and in separation from Him. Its main purpose is to speak to such rebels the word not of condemnation but of mercy, and to show to them God's provision of a way of full salvation in Christ. It is impossible to use Scripture properly as believers, unless we first accept its diagnosis of our condition and the condition of our fellows as fallen creatures and as sinners, and unless we then set ourselves to show active, responsive interest in what God has to teach us through it about His graciously provided way of redemption, present restoration, and heavenly destiny for all who will but respond to His word of salvation.

(viii) *Regard Christ, and particularly His two comings to earth, as the main biblical subject*. This is both the scope and the limit of divine revelation. 'The testimony of

Jesus is the spirit of prophecy' (Rev. 19:10). It all bears
witness to Him, and – note the unqualified human name
Jesus – to His coming as the Man to us, whether to save
or to judge. It is He and He alone who can say, 'it is written about me in the scroll. I desire to do your will, O my
God;' (see Ps. 40:7,8; Heb. 10:7). He is the great Subject
and final Agent of both revelation and redemption. He is
both the Apostle and High Priest of our Christian confession (Heb. 3:1) who came to men for God as His
Revealer, and has gone to God for us as our one all-suf-
ficient Reconciler.

The part of Scripture which is called 'the gospel',
recorded for our fuller enlightenment by four writers, is
the record of His incarnation, ministry, death, resurrection and ascension. In His historic work He is supremely
God's Word of Salvation. For God's Word is always
accompanied by and consummated in actual performance. See Num. 23:19. The accompanying written words
of Holy Scripture are in the Old Testament preparatory
and prophetic, in the 'four gospels' recording and
explanatory; and in the Acts, epistles and Apocalypse
more fully explanatory and applicatory, indicating the
full significance of the Word which had been spoken,
indicating its, or rather His, larger outworking in those
who respond to Him and become part of His fulfilment,
and indicating finally the sure and certain consummation of all things in this Christ Jesus the Lord, who
now shares the throne of Deity as both very God and
very Man, and shall come to judge both the living and
the dead.

Therefore, all biblical study should be centred in Him.
He is their cause. If His coming had not been first
intended and then fulfilled, there would have been no
written word of revelation. For the written word is but
the complement or reflection of the Living Word.

Without Him it has no *raison d'être*. It is, so to speak, the halo round His head in which His glory finds visible or intelligible, because verbal, expression. Just as it requires the whole church, which is His body, the blessed company of all faithful people, to give expression to His fullness in human life, so it requires the whole of the Bible to give expression to His fullness in human words, and to make it possible for all to learn the Truth as it is in Jesus.

Also, it is plain from the New Testament records that only when the Christ actually came were believing students of the Old Testament Scriptures able to piece together their manifold parts, and to see that, in spite of the apparently contradictory character of some, they all found their fulfilment in Him. Similarly, when He shall appear the second time, many prophecies in both the Old and New Testament, which many cannot yet fully piece together (so that devout interpreters of prophecy do not all agree), will find their true unity and fulfilment in Him.

Christ and His two comings are, therefore, the key to the interpretation of Scripture. Prophecies can be understood only in the light of His appearing. The student should, therefore, make it his constant objective in all his study to see and learn through it more about Christ and His fullness.

(ix) *Recognize the progress and unity of the revelation as a whole, and the place and necessity for every part*. Regard the various books as coherent parts of a single system of God-given education for the human race. Recognize that each part has a contribution to make to full understanding, but that taken by itself in isolation it is incomplete and may even become misleading. Beware, therefore, of the tendency, so common in the critical approach, just to regard each book independently. We must not expect to be able to understand or appreciate it without reference to its place in relation to the rest. In practice this will mean that we take care to read the whole and not only favourite sections or selected portions. It will mean reading consecutively as well as undertaking a more analytical study of the details of particular sections. In other words study should be synthetic as well as analytic, comprehensive as well as selective.

(x) *Use the Old Testament as a preparation, background and virtual dictionary or book of reference for the understanding of the New Testament; and interpret the Old Testament in relation and subordination to the New Testament and to its own fulfilment in Christ.* It is clear that the New Testament writers believed that the Old Testament Scriptures were divinely intended to help them to understand the gospel of Jesus Christ, the Son of God; and their writings show that only in the light of what God did in the incarnation, death and resurrection of His Son, and the consequent gift of the Spirit, and the birth of a church which was to include all nations, can the true meaning and intention of many Old Testament passages and figures be understood. What is latent in the Old Testament is patent in the New.

The New is in the Old concealed,

The Old is in the New revealed.

Leviticus would be unsolved without Hebrews. So would Isaiah without the gospels. So would all the Bible without Christ.

(xi) *Compare verse with verse, and let the Bible check one's interpretation of the Bible.* See 1 Cor. 2:13. This rule follows as a necessary practical application of principles already enunciated. This is the only way to arrive at a true understanding both of it as a whole, and of the measure of truth in any particular part. Consistent obedience to this rule will mean that one passage of Scripture will not be so interpreted as to conflict with another. Such approach to the Bible is in strong contrast with the desire of some critical minds simply to look for apparent contradictions and to strive to show the apparent impossibility of loyalty to Scriptural truth by continually setting Scripture against Scripture. For such apparent opposites are deliberately intended to complement and counteract each other; and not to cancel each other out in pointless contradiction. Therefore, in this connection, any worthwhile Christian use of the word of revelation will be constructive and not destructive; it will increase insight and temper judgment and not uselessly confuse understanding.

(xii) *Aim to discover, and then to keep in harmony with, the general consent or tenor of the Bible.* A constant practical objective of all biblical study should be to get beyond the contributions of particular passages to a properly developed understanding of the consistent teaching as a whole. Heresies commonly start from an exaggerated interpretation of one side of truth. No error is more misleading than one which seems, to those who hold it, to be based on truth, or to be grounded in the Word of God. The only way to safeguard ourselves against such mistakes is to seek to keep within the circle of the Bible as a whole, and not to go off at a tangent from one or two passages on the circumference. This means that we must be willing to let the Bible alone continually confirm or correct our dearest convictions.

(xiii) *Recognize that the truth is many-sided.* There may be more than one aspect or point of view. For instance, humans are both mortal and immortal. Christ is both 'the Lion' and 'the Lamb' (Rev. 5:5,6). He is both the Lamb of God and the Shepherd of the flock of God. From one standpoint, that of the law (John 5:31), our Lord said, 'If I testify about myself, my testimony is not valid.' From another standpoint, that of His Person, He said, 'Even if I testify on my own behalf, my testimony is valid.' See John 5:31, 8:14.

(xiv) *Recognize the inevitable paradoxes of the truth about things infinite; and be prepared to accept both extremes.* Opposite aspects of infinite truth inevitably appear to finite minds to be contradictory and irreconcilable. Yet the humble and reverent student of divine revelation will recognize that 'the truth is not in the middle, and not in one extreme, but in both extremes'. Charles Simeon, whose words these are, added his own illustrations:

> Here are two extremes; observing days, eating meats, etc.

> "Paul, how do you move? In the mean way?"
> "No."
> "To one extreme?"
> "No."
> "How then?"
> "To both extremes in their turn, as occasion requires."

> Here are two other extremes, Calvinism and Arminianism (for you need not to be told how long Calvin and Arminius lived before St Paul).

> "How do you move in reference to these, Paul? In a golden mean?"
> "No."

"To one extreme?"

"No."

"How then?"

"To both extremes; today I am a strong Calvinist, tomorrow a strong Arminian!" (*Charles Simeon*, by Handley G.C. Moule, p.77)

This attitude was so characteristic of Charles Simeon and he was so explicit in his declaration of it, that an extract from the preface to his *Horae Homileticae* seems worthy of quotation at length.

> The author is disposed to think that the Scripture system is of a broader and more comprehensive character than some very dogmatical theologians are inclined to allow; and that, as wheels in a complicated machine may move in opposite directions and yet subserve one common end, so may truths apparently opposite be perfectly reconcilable with each other and equally subserve the purposes of God in the accomplishment of man's salvation. The author feels it impossible to avow too distinctly that it is an invariable rule with him to endeavour to give to every portion of the Word of God its full and proper force, without considering what scheme it favours, or whose system it is likely to advance. Of this he is sure that there is not a decided Calvinist or Arminian in the world who equally approves of the whole of Scripture . . . who, if he had been in the company of St Paul whilst he was writing his epistles, would not have recommended him to alter one or other of his expressions.
>
> But the author would not wish one of them altered; he finds as much satisfaction in one class of passages as in another; and employs the one, he believes, as freely as the other.

(xv) *Recognize the limits of revelation.* It is a mistake to expect to be made wise beyond what is written. God is a God who hides Himself. 'The secret things belong to the LORD' (Deut. 29:29). In answer to a pressing question of His disciples Jesus simply answered, 'It is not for you to know' (Acts 1:7). With reference to the time of His coming, He said, 'No one knows about that day or hour' (Mark 13:32). It therefore becomes us to be humble, not to seek after knowledge which is too high for us, and honestly to admit both to ourselves and to others that there are many things which we do not and cannot know in this present life, in which we see only through a glass darkly, and at the best know only in part (1 Cor. 13:12). It is important, also, to recognize that the individual's insight into truth is limited by the measure of his own progress in understanding. The things written cannot be all revealed to the individual learner all at once. We have to grow in discernment and understanding. In a school it is, for instance, impossible to teach to eleven year olds subjects taught only to eighteen year olds. So Jesus said to His most intimate disciples, 'I have much more to say to you, more than you can now bear' (John 16:12, cf. Mark 4:33). Similarly He said to Peter, 'You do not realize now what I am doing, but later you will understand' (John 13:7). We must therefore recognize that our own personal moral condition and the measure of our spiritual growth also put a limit on what God can reveal to us through His Word.

(xvi) *Interpret the obscure by the clear and the partial by the more complete reference.* Some passages and statements of the Bible, taken by themselves and particularly on first acquaintance, are very obscure and hard to understand. Their language, too, may be figurative and enigmatic; they seem to need clarification. Others are so brief that they seem to need amplification. In such cases it is important to look for some clear and more detailed biblical statement as an aid to true understanding, and not to make incomplete or abstruse statements the main foundation of what, as far as the rest of the Bible is concerned, is a novel doctrine.

(xvii) *Remember not only that human understanding is at the best still finite., but also that individual ability to grasp the fullness of revealed truth is still more limited.* It is wrong to make the measure of our individual understanding a standard for deciding the meaning or judging the value of all parts of Scripture. There may be parts which will never come within the range of either my need or my appreciation. To take the extreme case, some passages may even be beyond the understanding of the age in which we live or the race and thought-world to which we belong. But that does not mean that they ought no longer to have a place in the book that was written for the edification of all ages and all races and to meet the needs of all kinds of people.

(xviii) *Respect the judgment of other believers, particularly the consensus of the saints.* It is self-deceiving and dangerous for anyone to imagine that he has a monopoly of the truth. In our study and exposition it is therefore wise to treat with respect interpretations held by others, particularly when such interpretations have for long been accepted by most if not all of God's people. As Russell Howden has said

> If, for instance, I find myself being led to a conclusion which is in conflict with some statement in the Apostles' Creed, I shall, if I am sensible, question the accuracy of my own conclusion and be inclined to think that the Creed may be correct and I mistaken.

Similarly, if I wish to increase my own understanding of the Bible, I shall do well to make a proper use of the real aid afforded by the many published commentaries and expositions, particularly when I know them to be the work of those of humble faith and consecrated scholarship.

Therefore do not be dogmatic in matters over which the equally devout disagree. Obviously there are some matters both of textual interpretation and of moral discernment on which it is not possible to arrive at one final judgment. There is something to be said from the Bible for more than one view. While, therefore, it may be good to decide one's personal viewpoint, it would be uncharitable and unjustifiable so to assert it among one's fellow Christians as to condemn those who hold some other view which experience shows to be equally possible.

(xix) *Seek the enlightenment and testimony of the Holy Spirit.* This is, of course, of primary and universal importance. It is only by the illumination of the Spirit that we can discern, and only by His sanction or witness that we can know the certainty of revealed truth. The Holy Spirit has been given for this purpose, to reveal things otherwise beyond our thoughts or imagination, and to give us the confidence or assurance of a sure and certain faith. He is the only Teacher fully able to expound His own inspired textbook of holy learning. If, therefore, we would use the Bible to full advantage we ought to do it in an attitude of conscious and continually renewed dependence upon the Holy Spirit.

5

Interpreting the Text: Special Rules

1. Figurative language

Figurative language is a common feature of the Bible, which clearly needs to be properly appreciated and rightly interpreted. Help in doing this may be gained by a prior consideration of its chief characteristics and its main forms.

1. Its chief characteristics

(i) *Its universal character*. Such language is by no means peculiar to the Bible. It is a feature found in every language and in all expression of thought. It is natural to us to think about things and to describe them in this way. Also, in contrast to abstract and technical terms, this kind of thought-form is typical of the common people. It is a language used and understood by all. It is because the Bible uses such language so freely that it is so understandable by all types of people.

(ii) *Its governing principle*. This is, of course, the principle of comparison or analogy. We tend in all our speaking to describe one thing by reference to another, and in particular to describe the new and unfamiliar by comparison with the well known, which only has to be mentioned to awaken at once understanding and responsive appreciation.

(iii) *Its necessary use.* If we are to describe things at all we can do so only in terms of the known and in language already current. We must interpret significance within the thought-forms of our own actual experience. Many things divinely revealed are unseen or spiritual; or they are new and hitherto unconceived. The only way for their character and significance to be suggested to us is by the use of some corresponding figure taken from the seen and the familiar. Consequently God is spoken of anthropomorphically and heaven is always described figuratively. No other method of conveying any impression of the truth is available.

(iv) *Its positive value.* Figurative language makes an immediate and vivid appeal to the imagination. It calls up concrete pictures. It illuminates and illustrates by direct contact with actual experience and ordinary human interests. Also, it leaves a picture on the mind and memory which is calculated to remain and is easily capable of being recalled. It is, therefore, an indispensable method of teaching. So our Lord spoke to fishermen of becoming 'fishers of men', and to a woman at a well of drinking 'the water that I shall give'.

(v) *Its peculiar suitability.* The Bible teaches that in many ways there is a close correspondence between things natural and things spiritual. The one is often a reflection of the other. In particular, God made man in His own image and likeness. Therefore, the use of natural figures to strike a comparison is a form of language and of expression of thought made possible by the Creator Himself. Still more, it is finally demonstrated to be in harmony with God's chosen method of self-revelation, by the fact that He chose to reveal Himself to men and women within their world by Himself becoming man, and thus expressing the eternal, the spiritual and the divine in terms of the temporal, the natural and the human.

(vi) I*ts prominence in the Old Testament.* In the age before Christ came God prepared the minds of men to appreciate Christ's Person and His redemptive work by the use of 'figures of the true'. The divinely ordered history and the divinely ordained religious ritual of the Israelites form one grand 'type' or figure. As Augustine said, 'Novum Testanientum in Vetere latet, Vetus in Novo patet'. This whole preparatory dispensation was 'the shadow of good things to come'. It was providentially designed to resemble and to prepare for the reality to follow. Therefore the reader of the Old Testament should expect to find things figurative, and ought to seek to acquire skill in their right interpretation.

(vii) *Dangers of false interpretation.* These scarcely need stating. Analogy is calculated only to mislead those who mistake comparison for proof. Also, history shows how great is the danger in case devout interpreters of Scripture should run to extravagant excess not only in the interpretation of figurative language, but also in the fancied discovery of allegorical meanings in what are originally non-figurative statements. It is unwise to allow oneself to become fascinated by the desire to find mysteries hidden in some fanciful way beneath the plain record of history. It is unbalanced to claim to find by figurative interpretation more spiritual teaching in an obscure passage or in one whose surface meaning seems to have little which concerns us than in passages whose relevant doctrinal truth or moral exhortations are as plain as day. Also the heretics' use of the Bible shows how easy it is by allegorizing to make the Bible teach heresy instead of orthodox doctrine.

2. Its main forms

(i) *Simple figures or word pictures.* These are common in all languages. They abound in the Bible, and provide a fascinating study. In the simile there is an explicit comparison, e.g. Ps. 103:13, 'As a father has compassion on his children, so the LORD has compassion on those who fear him'. In the metaphor words of description are transferred to objects to which they are not originally and literally applicable; there is an implicit comparison, e.g. Eph. 2:19,20, 'Consequently, you are no longer foreigners and aliens, but fellow citizens with God's people and members of God's household, built on the foundation of the apostles and prophets, with Christ Jesus   himself as the chief cornerstone.'

(ii) *Projected figures or imaginative representations*, which exist only in the imagination. Such are obviously meant to signify more than they literally say. Often they are incapable of literal interpretation. But they serve to represent to the mind actual truth, quality, character, etc. They are particularly used to present an impression of things which are beyond direct concrete representation, e.g. heaven. To this class belong the fable, and the apocalypse. Examples are Judg. 9:7–15; where the trees are represented as seeking a king; Ps. 80:8–16, which describes how God brought a vine out of Egypt and planted it, etc.; Dan. 2:31–35, the account of Nebuchadnezzar's dream;

the visions of the Apocalypse such as Rev. 21:21, where we are told that the street of the city was pure gold.

(iii) *Quasi-historical stories or parables*, which keep within the limits of the human and the possible. These are stories from nature or human life which secure interest for their own sake, but which need interpretation if their real significance is to be appreciated. Examples are the story of the poor man's ewe lamb (2 Sam. 12:1–4) and Jesus' parables.

(iv) *Actual events, individuals, objects, etc., which can be interpreted typically or allegorically* as having some special figurative significance. For example, features which are due to providential ordering and supernatural intervention, like the Jewish sacrificial ritual or Jesus' miracles, are clearly intended to be regarded as 'types' or 'signs'. Also, certain objects in the Bible, e.g. the Lord's anointed, the holy city, come to stand for an ideal conception, which is projected beyond the thing primarily referred to. So Jerusalem is ultimately 'from above', the heavenly city, the metropolis of all the people of God. Thus such objects not only become 'figures of the true' but provide names or thought-forms by means of which 'the true' may be conceived, appreciated, and expressed by human minds. So Jesus, the Son of God, is 'the Christ' (i.e. the anointed one). Similarly He is 'the true vine'.

3. Rules for the interpretation of figurative language

(i) *Figurative language needs to be clearly recognized and treated as such.* This means that when language is purely figurative it ought not to be taken literally, or one may be led into grievous errors of thought. It is wrong to expect either to see here the devil literally as a roaring lion

(1 Pet. 5:8), or to see in heaven our Saviour literally as a Lamb in the midst of the throne (Rev. 5:5). If our Lord's words about the broken bread, 'This is my body' (compare 'All men are like grass', Isa. 40:6) were to be taken literally, there would at once appear to be biblical ground for belief in the doctrine of transubstantiation. To such an extent is it true that figurative language is not to be taken literally, that it is possible figuratively to accept both of two statements which as literal facts would be mutually exclusive. For example

> In Ps. 18:11 God is said to make 'darkness his covering', and in 1 Tim. 6:16 He is said to 'live in unapproachable light'. In the first case darkness means inscrutableness, and in the second light means purity, intelligence, or honour. In Ex. 33:11 it is said that God 'would speak to Moses face to face', and in verse 20 He declares that no man can see His face and live. In the first passage the expression means to have intercourse without the intervention of another; in the second, to have a full and familiar sight of the divine glory. (Angus, *Bible Handbook*, p. 218)

(ii) *Such language needs and deserves special study*, particularly in order to appreciate references which are not familiar to our unenlightened and more matter-of-fact Western minds. The East is the home of flowery and figurative language. The Bible abounds in figurative references to Eastern customs and surroundings. These make its descriptions very vivid and picturesque. But often they are completely unappreciated by the English reader – like windows of which the blinds have never been drawn to let in the light. For example, the Bible idea of 'a dog' is something completely different from ours. So much so that Rev. 22:15 says of the heavenly city, 'Outside are the dogs, those who practise magic arts . . .

and murderers, etc.' In Ps. 59:6 David says of his enemies, 'They return at evening, snarling like dogs, and prowl about the city.' For in many places in the East the following is true.

> All day long the dogs are driven out from human habitations and forage for themselves in the open country, but as night draws on they steal back under the cover of darkness, and savagely growl at one another as they fight for their food, and at all strange passers-by, forming indeed a striking and appropriate image of the wicked. (*Strange Figures or the Figurative Language of the Bible*, James Neill, pp. 17, 18)

Contrast the word our Lord used to the Syro-Phoenician woman. He said, 'It is not meet to take the children's bread, and cast it to the little dogs' (literally 'puppies', a diminutive; Mark 7:27).

> For "dog" in the East is an awful term of contempt . . . "Dogs" are never allowed in the houses, never stroked by the master, never fed by the children, but "little dogs" or "puppies" are. So the woman was encouraged to answer, "Lord, but even the puppies under the table eat of the children's crumbs!" (Neill, pp. 26, 27)

(iii) *Make a special study of biblical usage*. There are some figures which are wholly peculiar to the Bible and to people schooled in the language of the prophets and messengers of God. In the Bible some words come by origin and usage to have a particular meaning and significance, which can be appreciated only by those who are prepared to use the Bible as its own dictionary. They form, in fact, the language of Zion, which none understand except those who are 'born in Zion' (see Ps. 87). For instance, our Lord's words first about Nathanael, and then to him, can be understood only in the light of God's dealings with Jacob. To understand 'Here is a true Israelite, in whom there is nothing false' (or no 'Jacob', John 1:47) one must have read 'Your name will no longer be Jacob, but Israel' (Gen. 32:28), and one must know the meaning of 'Jacob' (see Gen. 27:36). Also, to understand John 1:51 one must be familiar, as Nathanael was, with the story of Gen. 28:10–19.

In this connection it is particularly important to make a special study of words and ideas, which are prepared in the Old Testament in order to provide a vocabulary and thought-forms with which express and to interpret the blessings of the gospel of Christ. Here is a selection only of such words: the Lord's Messiah, the city of God, the people of God, the Israel of God, the seed of Abraham, the Ecclesia or church, the Passover, sacrifice, the blood of the covenant, shedding of blood, propitiation, ransom, entrance into the holiest, the true 'Sabbath' or rest of the people of God, the day of the Lord. Serious students, who wish to let the Bible become its own interpreter, should add to this list for themselves, and in each case seek to find out the ultimate Christian significance of such figures of speech.

(iv) *Interpret by careful reference to the context* in order to discover the direction and limitations within which the figure is to be applied and understood. Because figurative statements are not literal ones they cannot rightly be quoted in isolation as if by themselves they made a complete declaration of truth. Their use and purpose are to illuminate and describe. They can fulfil this function only when they are properly related to their subject like an adjective to the noun which it qualifies. For example, when Hosea (4:10–19, 5:3,4) speaks of Israel's lasciviousness and adultery it is clear from the context that he means not sexual immorality but departure from the Lord and devotion to idols.

4. The place and use of allegorical interpretation of historical narratives, etc.

(i) *Such practice is justified and encouraged by Scriptural example and precedent*. There are places in the New Testament where passages from the Old Testament are treated in this way. For instance, Paul sees in Hagar and Sarah and in their two sons Ishmael and Isaac a picture of the two covenants, the old covenant of the Law and the better covenant of promise. And he says explicitly that these things are an allegory (Gal. 4:21–31). Similarly he says that the injunction in the law not to muzzle the ox that treads out the corn was written for our learning and makes plain that the Lord has ordained that they that preach the gospel should live of the gospel (1 Cor. 9:7–14).

(ii) *Such practice is necessary in order to discover the highest significance and the true spiritual teaching of some subjects and passages*. For example: by this method of interpretation the Melchizedek of Gen. 14:17–20 is in Heb. 7:1–10 regarded as 'made like unto the Son of God' (KJV). Similarly in Eph. 5:22–33, when Paul talks of the relationship of husbands and wives, he says that its highest significance can be understood only if it is applied to or interpreted by the relationship between Christ and the church. The Song of Solomon is a still more outstanding example. If this Song is taken literally it refers only and completely to human love between a man and a woman. The name of God is not mentioned. There are no words of explicit religious sentiment whatever. Yet both the Jewish and the Christian churches have thought this

song worthy of a place in the canon, because allegorically interpreted it gives rich insight into the depth of
intimacy and love in the relationship between God and
His chosen people and between Christ and His church.
Nor is such interpretation just arbitrary conjecture. It is
justified in principle by an obvious correspondence. Just
as human life finds its highest fulfilment in the love of
man and woman, so the supreme thing in religion is love
between the soul and God. Consequently the Song that
gives worthy expression to the delights of human love is
by analogy rightly taken as providing some picture of
the joys of communion between the people of God and
their Maker and Redeemer.

(iii) *Such practice needs to be employed only with great
restraint and, wherever possible, with confirming biblical justification.* Otherwise it gives unlimited scope to arbitrary
conjecture, and opens the door for people to read into
the Bible almost anything they wish to see there. When
there is, as in the example just given above (i.e. in the
interpretation of the Song of Solomon), some clear correspondence, particularly if it is a correspondence or
'figure of the true' which the Bible itself explicitly uses
elsewhere, then allegorical interpretation seems definitely justified. But it is unwise to imagine that on one's
own individual responsibility one can see figures there,
which no one else may have ever imagined to be present. It is healthier to keep to the plain, literal,
straight-forward meaning of the text.

5. Rules of general application to the interpretation of all which is regarded as Figurative – including parables

Whenever allegorical interpretation is allowed, the following general rules should be carefully observed.

(i) *Seek explicit biblical authority for the interpretation* or application of types, figures and parables. The mere perception of analogy will not suffice. One must make sure independently that the idea which one uses the figure to illustrate is God's truth, and that the consequent teaching based on it is in harmony with the general consensus of Bible teaching and with some orthodox system of biblical theology. For instance, we have Jesus' own authority for using the story of Num. 21:6–9 about 'the bronze snake' to illustrate the gospel truth that 'there is life for a look at the Crucified One'. See John 3:14,15.

(ii) *Never make a figure or a figurative interpretation the main basis of a doctrine or an article of faith.* Such doctrines should be built only on direct statements of Scripture. A figure is in character additional and illustrative. It cannot without the corresponding reality prove the existence of that which it may suggest or seem to mirror. Ultimately, it should be used only to illustrate realities which are known to exist independently, even if in some cases the first thing which makes some seekers look for the reality may be the suggestion in the figure. The types of the Old Testament were not fully appreciated until they were fulfilled. It is the independent discovery of the reality which justifies one in believing that the suggestion of the figure may be accepted.

(iii) *Concentrate attention on the central point or main truth which is illustrated by the figure.* Keep all the details subordinate to the main impression of the picture as a whole. Does not let interest in 'the trees' prevent you from seeing 'the wood'. In all figurative representations there is inevitably much that is mere costume or setting; it is the general truth that is to be examined and explained.

(iv) *Do not (except in special cases) attempt to find a spiritual significance in every detail*. Detailed correspondence should not be pursued without very clear biblical justification. Note that occasionally Jesus did do it, e.g. in interpreting the parables of the Sower, and of the Wheat and the Tares. See Matt. 13:3–9,18–23,24–30,36–43. But note, on the other hand, that when He told the parable of the Good Samaritan He used it simply to enforce one obvious lesson, i.e. how to fulfil the command to love one's neighbour as oneself. So He applied it not by explanation of its details, but by the one challenging injunction, 'Go and do likewise.' See Luke 10:25–37. Note further that there are some parables in which it is quite impossible, and would indeed become blasphemous, to attempt to find correspondence in every detail; for example in the parable of the Friend at Midnight (Luke 11:5–10).

(v) *Avoid over-imaginative interpretations* which entertain rather than convict, and which tend in consequence to distract attention from the main lesson and practical moral challenge of the passage. Such interpretations far from being helpful are – like fables and endless genealogies (1 Tim. 1:4) – definitely unhelpful.

(vi) *Keep all interpretations strictly subordinate to the highest spiritual ends*. Concentrate on figures and interpretations which clearly illustrate important spiritual truths and which have a direct moral bearing on daily life and conduct.

2. Prophecy

Before indicating any rules of interpretation it seems desirable to consider the essential character of prophecy, its purpose, and its special value.

1. Some general considerations

(i) *Its character*. Just as miracles are works of divine omnipotence, so prophecy is essentially the word of divine omniscience. In prophecy the inspired spokesman gives utterance to special, extraordinary and supernatural knowledge. In its widest embrace such knowledge may concern the past, the present, or the future. The prophet is someone of God-given backsight, insight, or foresight. The prophet declares the real truth about what was, or is, or is to be. Because announcement about the future is the most obviously remarkable, though not necessarily the most important or most valuable of the utterances of the prophet, the word prophecy is often applied to this particular type alone. It is such predictive prophecy that we are here more particularly to consider.

(ii) *Its purpose*. This is to make plain to us the ways of God, and to disclose something of the meaning and consummation of history as He sees and controls it. The purpose of predictive prophecy is to make us aware of what God will do and how He will act, and thus to indicate to us what they may most certainly expect and anticipate. It has, therefore, an immediate practical relevance to the present. Its purpose is to provide people with two things – first a sure ground of confidence how God will act, and second a compelling moral indication how they should act. Its purpose is to move to repentance and obedience because of certain judgment, and to provide encouragement and inspire hope because of coming redemption. It is meant, therefore, to indicate to people what they ought to do or how they ought to be living now. Jesus ended His great eschatological discourse with a practical application and a present imperative, 'What I say to you, I say to everyone: 'Watch!' (Mark 13:37)

Predictive prophecy has a further relevance to the time of the ultimate fulfilment of God's will in history. By preparing people's minds, by making them aware how He works, and how He is pleased to intervene, God qualifies some to recognize and rightly to receive such action when it occurs. Those who intend to visit a place where they have friends whose co-operation they desire commonly write to them beforehand to say when and why they will be coming, or, maybe, by what premonitory signs their near approach may be recognized. So God does not hide from His friends the things which He will do. Rather, as Amos wrote, 'Surely the Sovereign LORD does nothing without revealing his plan to his servants the prophets.' See Gen. 18:17 and Amos 3:7.

(iii) *Its evidential value.* If an intending visitor writes beforehand a letter to friends indicating in detail things he intends to do when he comes; and then later he actually comes and one by one does these very things, two deductions may be made. First, the fulfilment proves the genuineness of the letter; unquestionably it was an expression of his mind. Second, the fulfilment proves the identity and the good faith of the individual; here obviously is none other than the author of the letter carrying out in person his own declared intention. Note, too, that the fulfilment of the details is not compelled by the statements previously made in the letter. Rather it proves that these statements were made by the fulfiller, and made in good faith, as a declaration of his already conceived intention.

Similarly, the fulfilment of predictive prophecy is the foremost proof appealed to in the Bible that the word of the prophet is of God. See Deut. 18:21,22; Isa. 41:21–23.

Fulfilment of predictive prophecy has this double evidential value. It indicates the divine origin, inspiration and authority of the Bible. Also, it vindicates the identity of the Fulfiller. By His fulfilment of prophecy Jesus is demonstrated to be both Lord and Christ. For example, note that Jesus predicted His own resurrection, and that the fulfilment of His prophecy demonstrated both the trustworthiness of His words and the identity of His person as the Christ, the Son of God.

2. Rules for its right interpretation

(i) *Recognize that God's special preparatory providences as recorded in the Old Testament were often themselves predictive or prophetic.* They were samples of His ways. They were 'figures of the true' and 'shadows of the good things to come'. This is the justification for the figurative or allegorical interpretation of Old Testament passages, by which some individuals, objects, incidents, ceremonies, etc., are regarded as types or predictive anticipations of the great things of Christ and the gospel. The prediction is not merely in words, but in the whole pattern of the history. It is a declaration or suggestion beforehand of the way in which the same God will one day work to bless all in Christ. So, for example, Joseph in his rejection by his brothers and in his exaltation from humiliation to be the supplier of food and preserver of life not only to his brothers but also to the Egyptians, may surely be regarded as an anticipation in outline of the Son of David, who, rejected by Israel, has been exalted to be the Saviour of the world.

(ii) *Seek fast to appreciate each prophecy in its original setting and primary application.* Endeavour to find out what it meant at the time to its original author and to its first hearers. For the prophets were not only messengers for all time. They were also men of their own time. They spoke first in and to their own generation. The student ought, therefore, to seek to understand what they said in its reference and relation to their immediate historical circumstances. Such historical understanding of the original meaning is the starting point and necessary preliminary for all larger understanding.

(iii) *Recognize the possibility of further reference or larger significance*. While the immediate meaning should be appreciated first, the student who believes in God's inspiration of the prophets to write for our learning and not merely for their contemporaries will also be ready to believe that the same words may have a second or ultimate significance. It is this significance which makes the words fully predictive. They are an indication not only of the way in which God will work in one particular setting but also of how He will work in relation to humanity as a whole. They may indicate, for instance, some aspect of the pattern either of God's supreme intervention to save, or of His final consummation of all things in judgment. So they are a prophecy either of Christ's First Advent or of His Second Advent.

(iv) *Recognize the particular character of the language used*. Because prophecy deals with events outside the experience or world of the human authors, it tends of necessity to use figures and symbols, and sometimes to be cast in a kind of language of its own which is somewhat poetic, and full of symbolic details which can scarcely all be taken literally, but are nevertheless the recognized associated features of the anticipated consummation. The following are examples of this special phraseology: 'the sun will be darkened, and the moon will not give its light; the stars will fall from the sky'; 'the Son of man sitting at the right hand of the Mighty One, and coming on the clouds of heaven'; 'the trumpet will sound'; 'with a loud command, with the voice of the archangel and with the trumpet call of God'. See Mark 13:24, 14:62; 1 Cor. 15:52; 1 Thes. 4:16. Sometimes, too, the wording may be loose enough to permit a slightly different second meaning, a meaning of which the prophet was probably unaware or which he did not primarily intend, but which can be given to his utterance without any corruption being done to the naturalness of what he said in its original setting. See, for example, John 11:49–52.

In illustration of this and the previous two rules see Isa. 7:14, 'The virgin will be with child and will give birth to a son, and will call him Immanuel.' These words obviously had an immediate reference. For the child to be born was to be a sign to the people of that day. Before the child became old enough to distinguish good from evil the two enemies of Judah were to be overthrown (Isa. 7:16). In this connection the prophecy made no reference to miraculous virgin birth or to divine incarnation. It simply meant that a young woman – possibly a particular one ('the virgin'), say a princess of the royal household, and possibly one not yet married but about to be – would give birth to a son, and would express her faith in God and in the certainty of His help by calling the child 'Immanuel'. This would be her way of declaring in dark and perilous times her confidence that God was on their side (contrast 1 Sam. 4:19–22); and her faith was not to be disappointed. In Matt. 1:22,23, the same words of prophecy are taken to have a second and more extraordinary meaning. Here 'Emmanuel' becomes literally true in the person of the child. He Himself is 'God with us'. Also, here 'the virgin' is, as the original might mean but did not ordinarily imply, still an unmarried woman, even when the child was born. The birth of this child was the greatest of all God-given signs of deliverance from our enemies. Therefore this was the true fulfilment or ideal realization of the word of the prophet.

(v) *Recognize that the language often becomes figurative and allegorical in its wider prophetic application.* This means that references which were originally literal come in their adapted prophetic use to have a symbolic significance. For instance, Sodom, Egypt and Babylon are literal places in Old Testament history and symbolic figures in the Apocalypse. See Rev. 11:8 and 14:8. Mount Zion is in the New Testament a name for heaven itself, i.e. the heavenly Jerusalem. Heb. 12:22; Gal. 4:26; Rev. 14:1 and 21:2: cf. Isa. 2:2–4; Mic. 4:1–7.

(vi) *Recognize the limits of revelation.* Many things are not made known. Be humble enough to accept these limitations. Do not try to satisfy an unhealthy curiosity. It is a serious misuse of the Bible to try to make it disclose more than God has purposed to reveal. For instance, our Lord made plain that it was not for us, not even for His most intimate followers, to know the times and seasons, which the Father has set within His own authority (Acts 1:7, and also see Mark 13:32 and Deut. 29:29).

(vii) *Recognize the possibility of varying and mistaken interpretations.* Do not claim infallibility as an interpreter. Words which have more than their original literal meaning and are intended to serve as a revelation of eternal and final truth may well stand and need more than one finite interpretation to encompass all that they are meant to suggest of infinite fulfilment. Varying interpretations may each have in them some elements of truth. Also, the undeniable fact that the most prayerful believers have differed in their interpretations is itself witness that this is a field in which none can claim to speak the last word. It is only the central facts and general principles of God's activity of which we can be absolutely sure. It does not suit us to claim to know in exact detail God's programme. While the predictions concerning Christ's First Advent were all fulfilled in detail, the way of their fulfilment was fully understood only in the light of the actual event. In Israel at the time of Jesus' coming, there were clearly varying interpretations of Messianic prophecy, and – we must notice – many of them were wrong!

(viii) *Recognize that the primary purpose of prophecy and of its interpretation is to reveal Christ*, and to enable us to learn of Him. Any study of this subject which is not clearly calculated to magnify Him and to promote His glory and His Kingdom ought to be abandoned for study that is.

(ix) *Remember always the practical moral purpose of the Word of revelation*. See again Deut. 29:29 and note especially its closing words 'that we may follow all the words of this law'. As has been already indicated, all study if it is to be really useful ought to have some direct practical bearing on present life and conduct. Beware of all merely theoretical interest which tends to divert attention from the main business of Christian living. Let's seek to be doers of the word and not interpreters only.

6

The Bible and Christian Living

One cannot stress too often that the matter of first importance in all handling of the Bible is its immediate practical relevance both to the eternal destiny and to the present daily life and conduct of every individual. In conclusion, therefore, we will look at some practical rules for using the Bible, by following which we may hope to live lives more to God's glory and ourselves to enjoy the direct practical benefits which it has been written to make ours. See 2 Tim. 3:15–17.

(i) *Regard the Bible as a handbook of personal religion, a daily means of grace, and regularly use it as such.* God rewards all who diligently seek Him. He is the living God who still speaks by His Spirit to the seeking soul. He speaks in and through His written Word. I can, therefore, use the Bible as a present means of communion with God, and as a means by which I may, as I read it, expect Him to speak, and actually experience Him speaking to my soul, to enlighten, convict, assure, guide, restrain, encourage, etc.

This personal use of the Bible is one which the Reformers of the sixteenth century used by God to restore to the church. One cannot do better than quote from A History of the Reformation, by T.M. Lindsay.

All the Reformers of the sixteenth century, whether Luther, Zwingli, or Calvin, believed that in the Scriptures God spoke to them in the same way as He had done in earlier days to His prophets and apostles. They believed that if the common people had the Scriptures in a language which they could understand, they could hear God speaking to them directly, and could go to Him for comfort, warning or instruction; and their description of what they meant by the Holy Scriptures is simply another way of saying that all believers can have access to the very presence of God. The Scriptures were therefore for them a personal rather than a dogmatic revelation. They record the experience of a fellowship with God enjoyed by His saints in past ages, which may still be shared in by the faithful. In Bible history, as the Reformers conceived it, we hear two voices – the voice of God speaking love to man, and the voice of the renewed man answering in faith to God. This communion is no dead thing belonging to a bygone past; it may be shared here and now. (Vol. 1, p. 453)

(ii) *Let Scripture set the limit to revelation; but set no limit to what God can reveal through Scripture.* The Bible is the Christian's rule of faith. To know what to believe as Christians this book must be our decisive court of appeal. To quote the sixth of The 39 Articles of the Church of England

Holy Scripture containeth all things necessary to salvation: so that whatsoever is not read therein, nor may be proved thereby, is not to be required of any man, that it should be believed as an article of the Faith, or be thought requisite or necessary to salvation.

This means that we ought always to seek for biblical ground and justification for all our Christian faith and conduct. On the other hand, this never means, because the Bible is an ancient book, that we know all there is to know. None of us know all that the Bible has to teach. Always 'there remains yet much more light to break forth from God's Word'. God can use the same lasting Word to speak to us in new ways. Its truth and treasure are inexhaustible. We can rightly look to God to use it to give us fresh light for fresh needs. It is wrong, therefore, with regard to any matter to adopt the attitude that this is a subject on which the Bible cannot help me.

(iii) *Aim most to discover spiritual truth which is capable of immediate personal application.* Do not read the Bible merely as a detached spectator or enquiring student whose only concern is to know what it contains. Regard it rather as a looking-glass in which you can by God's help see both the person you are and the person you are meant to become as a child of God. Look first in it for the things which directly bear on your own needs and problems, failures and temptations, responsi-bilities and duties. Be prepared seriously and sincerely to ask, and to face the answer to pertinent questions. What has God to say to me today through this passage? What may I learn here concerning daily life, and how to live it to please God?

(iv) *Be a doer of the word and not a hearer only. See Jas 1:22–25.* In your study of the Bible expect to find yourself confronted over and over again with imperatives which demand active obedience and diligent and steadfast continuance in well-doing; and strive, by the help of God, to show your love to Him by keeping His commandments. Be like the man who built his house on the rock; and beware of being deceived into the false and foolish satisfaction of knowing without doing. See Matt. 7:24–27. Be on the look out continually for fresh things to do which the teaching of the Bible demands, but which you personally have never done before, or need to be stirred to do afresh.

(v) *Aim to know what the Bible teaches about God's way of salvation for sinners.* Concentrate first on essentials. Be sure you know and grasp clearly those revealed truths which are of primary importance for our eternal wellbeing. Seeing that Scripture is provided to make plain to men God's way of eternal salvation, aim to discover direct from the Bible itself exactly what Scripture does or does not teach on this momentous subject. For instance, 'salvation' in its full content has three stages, initial, progressive and final; also, it is enjoyed not alone but within a company of fellow believers. Aim, therefore, to discover what the Bible teaches about forgiveness or remission of sins, about sanctification or growth in holiness, about glorification or the consummation of bliss in the life beyond; and how these things can be enjoyed only in Christ and within the living fellowship of 'the church which is His body'.

(vi) *Strive to be prepared to give a biblical answer as a reason for the faith that is in you.* See 1 Pet. 3:15. Seek from the Bible to discover not only what Christians believe, but why, so that you may be able without hesitation to answer the questioner and to justify your Christian confidence. It is of no small importance to be able to quote or to appeal direct to the Bible in support of your assertions. This requires thoughtful understanding of what it does teach, so that you may use it to afford not a mere superficial pretext, but a sure and solid foundation for your faith.

(vii) *Aim to build up a systematic doctrinal belief or biblical theology.* As one's knowledge of the Bible increases one becomes able to collect and classify its teaching under a connected series of main subjects. Thus one can seek to arrive at a full and balanced appreciation of all that the Bible teaches on each particular subject. Such a method of study should also enable those who follow it properly to see the many truths of Scripture as one grand connected whole or consistent system, and not just as a string of disconnected fragments. When a new truth or a fresh aspect of a truth is seen in the Bible one should seek at once to connect it, and to give it its due place in relation to the rest of God's teaching, whether on this one truth, or on all the other complementary truths. This is true biblical theology – the understanding of the things of God as they are revealed for our learning in the divinely inspired textbook. 'Bonus theologus est bonus textuarius.' 'The good theologian is really only a good interpreter.'

(viii) *Aim to work out a practical moral code directly related to life and circumstances.* This does not mean meticulous and multitudinous rules. Emphasis should be placed rather on main guiding principles – the spirit of the law rather than the letter. But some attempt to discover and then to apply these principles is necessary if one is fully to use the Bible as a guide to right conduct. One should seek to decide in its light and from its teaching the kind of action which is either right or wrong, so that one may know how one ought to act to please God and to avoid sin. Here it is important to remember that one individual or community cannot even from God's Word lay down the law in every detail for other individuals or communities. Just as circumstances, social conditions and individual characteristics and qualifications continually differ, so detailed application of divine truth continually varies. Everyone must be fully persuaded in their own mind. One should exercise oneself to have a conscience void of offence. Whatsoever is not of faith is sin. See Acts 24:16; Rom. 14:5,14,22,23.

(ix) *Recognize the place of individual conscience and judgment.* This follows from what has just been said. For the Bible speaks fully to all only according to the measure of their entrance into light; and that is the point at which they must respond to its further challenge if they are to progress in its understanding. What is right for one may be wrong for another. See 1 Corinthians 8:4 and 7. Each must follow the light as they see it. So, as we have seen in time of war, it may be possible for some Christians to refuse to take up arms, and others, with equal conscientiousness and appeal to the Bible, to regard it as their duty to fight. One must be fully persuaded in one's own mind. And since, in a sinful world, neither can be wholly right, each may be making his contribution and giving his witness to further God's will and God's glory among others.

(x) *Recognize the need for continual return to, and fresh reformation according to, the Word of God.* This pursuit first of the discovery and then of the doing of God's will as revealed through His Word never ends. In this life we never reach the place of final perfection. Each fresh day brings its fresh challenge. The road is uphill all the way. It is all too easy to degenerate and to slip back from the observance of standards once accepted. No one reformation can put an individual or a church permanently right. There is constant need for a continual return to God to examine oneself afresh in the light of His Word, to be convicted of the beginnings of sinful decline, to be made aware of fresh ways in which advance in holiness and love is now possible. Only so can we follow on to know God, and hope to share in coming 'to a perfect man'. We must be willing always to submit ourselves to the searching light and compelling imperatives of the Word of God. 'The sacrifices of God are a broken spirit; a broken and a contrite heart, O God, you will not despise' (Ps. 51:17).

(xi) *Recognize that the person whom everyone is responsible to judge in this light is their own self.* Such practical moral application of the Bible to life and conduct is something which each believer is called and qualified in Christ to do alone. This is our Christian calling to grow up from infancy to full adult responsibility as members of God's family; not to be permanently subject to 'tutors and governors' but to arrive at a responsible mind of our own as Christian men and women. Then with such a mind our first responsibility is not to seek to compel others to conform to our reading of the Bible, nor to criticize them for failing to do so, but rather to submit ourselves to the criticism and constraint of this standard. 'But if we judged ourselves, we would not come under judgment' (1 Cor. 11:31). 'Anyone, then, who knows the good he ought to do and doesn't do it, sins' (Jas 4:17). '"Not everyone who says to me, 'Lord, Lord,' will enter the kingdom of heaven, but only he who does the will of my Father who is in heaven"' (Matt. 7:21).

(xii) *Never stop seeking to make further progress in understanding and obedience.* No individual in this earthly pilgrimage ever reaches the place where one understands all, or has done all that God requires of His children. Rather you are like an explorer confronted by limitless territory of which there always still remains much more yet to be possessed. It never becomes any of us, there-fore, to relax our quest as though we had arrived at full knowledge or perfect performance. There are always room and need to discover more, and then to walk in the fresh light gained to God's greater glory. We are not to reckon ourselves to have understood completely. We are continually to be reaching forward like people in hot pursuit of fuller comprehension. So shall we, by God's grace, be among the company who 'follow on to know the Lord'.

Expounding God's Word

Some principles and methods

Contents

1

A Personal Testimony

The immediate aim of this book is to indicate and illustrate some principles and methods of biblical exposition. Its ultimate aim is to encourage you, the reader, to become a diligent and effective worker in the same field of ministry.

The first prerequisite in all such work is to get at the meaning of the written Word, to understand what it says, to appreciate what God by His Spirit is saying to us through it today. The governing principles of such right understanding are dealt with in *Understanding God's Word*, and so will not be repeated here.

The distinctive associated concern of the biblical expositor is to set forth this truth or revelation from God, discerned through the study of His written Word, in language understandable to the hearer or reader. The true expositor or expository preacher must 'deliver the goods' at the door of the audience's circumstance and need. They must discover by God's help how to present and apply the biblical statements in such a way that they become the living, relevant, meaningful Word of God, to the present-day hearer. Such declaration and exposition of the truth of divine revelation are the dominant interest of this additional volume. I hope God will use it to set some who read it on the same road of ministry to which He called me.

Here personal testimony concerning one's own beginnings may be helpful for some to hear. I will recount, therefore, my earliest attempts at biblical exposition.

Through contact with the Children's Special Service Mission as a boy, I not only joined the Scripture Union and became a daily reader of the Bible myself, but, at the age of twelve, I also started a Scripture Union branch and got others of my own age to join. When I was fourteen, Edmund Clark, finding I was a Scripture Union branch secretary, suggested that, as a local fellow-worker, I should read the Scripture Union portion one day at a C.S.S.M. beach service. This meant being expected to make some brief comment on the passage read. I decided that I was willing to try. But I was far too nervous to say so. A fortnight went by before Mr Clark mentioned the matter again. In case he should ask me, I had been overnight preparing myself each day to speak, if asked, on the Scripture passage next morning! So I was 'ready' when at last the opportunity came. Not that those who heard my first attempt benefited from what I said. But I benefited from the discipline of such preparation. I learnt from these early beginnings to expect God to give me some word from Himself from a passage not arbitrarily chosen by me, but independently given.

This same kind of discipline later became a regular feature of my life at school. When I was sixteen I shared in starting a short meeting, held for ten minutes on three mornings each week before lessons began. At this meeting there were brief opening and closing prayers, the Scripture Union portion for the day was read, and some comment was made on it. While the meetings were quite well attended, no other boy wanted the task of leading them. So for two years between the ages of sixteen and eighteen, I carried this responsibility alone. Three times a week I had to stand before my friends, and seek to show to them that, from a Bible passage fixed by others, God had something to say to us all. So it was – using figurative language understandable to those familiar with the Bible – that I came to believe and to prove that, when He breaks them, the Lord can do more with five loaves to feed the needy, than men can do with a hundred pounds' worth of bread. So, on each occasion, I looked to the Saviour to break down the passage, and to make what I might get out of it helpful to me, and suitable to share with others. Nor did I have the aid of printed notes on the passages of the kind that is available now.

My testimony is that the amazing possibilities of biblical exposition can be discovered simply and only by becoming Jesus' humble fellow-worker in active ministry to others, and by trusting Him from any particular passage to give one spiritual food to minister to those whom one is responsible to feed.

During the same period, when I was seventeen, I 'discovered', and was greatly struck by, 1 Corinthians 14: here I found an injunction to covet spiritual gifts, especially to prophesy (see verses 1, 12 and 19.) In the light of other statements in the chapter I understood prophesying to mean, not foretelling the future, nor receiving new revelations from heaven, but expounding revealed truth in a manner both intelligible and helpful to the hearer. Such an exposition should be related to our condition, and should be expressed in words which they can understand. Its aim should be to bring to the hearers instruction, challenge and encouragement (see verse 3).

So I began as a boy of seventeen to pray for this gift, and – on each occasion when I expounded God's Word – to pray for the grace to exercise the gift to the glory of God and the blessing of others. Such prayers I have continued often to pray since; and I can humbly testify that God has answered my prayers. My further prayer now is that He will lead others, who read this testimony, along the same path of ministry 'in the church' or 'congregation' where people gather to worship God, and to hear His Word.

2

Our Stewardship of God's Word

The place of the Bible in God's purpose

As an expositor of God's Word, as a man with the Bible as his constant authoritative textbook, the Christian preacher or teacher has something unique to offer. It is not only his privilege, but also his responsibility, to proclaim that God has acted in human history, both to reveal Himself, and to redeem humankind. So his gospel for all ought not to be founded in human philosophy and in ideas formed by the world, nor in his own personal preferences and prejudices, but in the faithful declaration of God's self-revealing and saving acts.

These acts of God, because they are acts in history, possess the character of particularity and once-for-allness. God is not repeating them either in each fresh generation or in every continent. If, therefore, they are to fulfill their universal and age-long purpose of speaking to all humankind, and bringing to every land light and hope, it is indispensable that they should be appropriately recorded, suitably interpreted and effectively announced. Nor has God left such necessary complementary ministries to chance. Prophets and apostles, each in their proper time, have been raised up of God to provide both the record and the interpretation of His interventions in history; and preachers and teachers are continually being called of God to proclaim and expound the Word of God entrusted to them in living application to the lives of their contemporaries – and all under the enlightenment of the inspiring Spirit.

'Surely the Sovereign LORD does nothing without revealing his plan to his servants the prophets'; so Amos saw. 'The Sovereign LORD has spoken—who can but prophesy?'; so Amos spoke (Amos 3:7–8). Such particular confessions indicate and illustrate the general method of divine revelation. God's special acts in history to reveal and to redeem have also been accompanied by the raising up of prophets to record and to interpret. Their words, fixed in permanent written form, are for all subsequent generations doubly indispensable. Without them the acts of God would not be fully known. Still more, without them the acts of God would never be understood and appreciated in all their unique and supernatural significance. So their words had to be uttered and preserved in writing. And their words still need to be read and expounded, else the very truths which God Himself has spoken or made known to men and women will not be heard or discerned by them.

What was true of the preparatory disclosures of God in Old Testament times, when He spoke to men 'by divers portions and in divers manners', here a little and there a little, is still more true of the crowning act of revelation, and the final work of redemption, through the incarnation and crucifixion of God the Son. Through specially chosen witnesses God, acting in sovereign providence, enabled the writing down of records of these events of revelation and redemption in ways which throw into relief their divine significance. For those who make response to Christ, and become His disciples, God similarly gave us in the epistles the set-ting out in writing of a fuller interpretation of the truths concerning God and humankind. The inspired writings therefore provide for such disciples a manifold indica-tion, both of the dynamic outworking of the benefits of this gospel in people's lives, and of the final consumma-tion in which it will inevitably issue at the end of history and in the life beyond. In this way was the New Testament added to the Old.

It is through these Testaments, and through these alone, that the true God can now be known and His sav-ing purposes for us discerned. Here only can we find the true Christ in both His divine Person and His saving work. To quote Alan Richardson

> The Christian understanding of historical revelation is that it was given through certain historical events as interpreted by the faith and insight of the prophets and apostles of the Bible . . . Christians believe that the perspective of biblical faith enables us to see very clearly and without distortion the biblical facts as they really are . . . The interpretation of the biblical facts, as it was given to them by those who recorded them in the biblical history and apostolic witness, is necessary to a true seeing of the facts themselves. (*Christian Apologetics*, pp. 92, 105)

What is more, it is God's further associated purpose that in each fresh generation and in every Christian congre-gation this written testimony should fulfill its illuminat-ing and saving ministry among humankind through the confirming witness of God the Spirit, and through the Spirit-enabled exposition and relevant practical applica-tion of the written Word by the faithful preacher or teacher. So these three should agree in one common wit-ness to convince and assure the hearer – the written

Word, the illuminating Spirit and the faithful preacher.
Also, since the Bible preacher is the divinely-appointed
'voice' to give the truth living utterance, or since the
Bible teacher is the divinely-intended expositor to make
the truth meaningful in relation to life, if the teacher
does not fall into proper line in ministry, not only is the
Word of God not heard, but listeners are compelled to
hear a disappointing counterfeit. 'The hungry sheep
look up and are not fed.'

Every Christian preacher or teacher, therefore, who
would faithfully fulfill his ministry, ought to recognize,
first, that he is called to serve God and to promote God's
glory and the listeners' good by preaching and teaching
Christ; second, that he is called to serve Christ, and to
present Him truly and fully by preaching and teaching
that Word which has been written so that all may know
Him; third, that he is called to serve God the Spirit by
seeking His illumination and following His guidance,
both in discovering within the written Word the truth of
God which is relevant, and in declaring its meaning and
application to the waiting audience; and, fourth, that he
is therefore called by the whole Trinity, Father, Son and
Spirit, to serve God by becoming a servant of the written
Word, a man whose utterances and teaching are wholly
determined by the written Word's plain statements, and
not by their own independent prejudices and preferences.

If only the many who have regular opportunities to
preach and to teach could be made to feel the amazing
wonder of their high privilege, and the full burden of
their solemn responsibility, as ministers of the God-
given Word. Then they would unquestionably give a
new priority to the discharge of their stewardship. Nor
is there any one thing that many groups of would-be
learners need more than the advent of a preacher or

teacher who, in the face of all the temptations to do otherwise, can but re-echo in principle the apostle Paul's words, 'Yet when I preach the gospel, I cannot boast, for I am compelled to preach. Woe to me if I do not preach the gospel! . . . I am simply discharging the trust committed to me.' (1 Cor. 9:16–17)

'So then, men ought to regard us as servants of Christ and as those entrusted with the secret things of God. Now it is required that those who have been given a trust must prove faithful.' (1 Cor. 4:1–2)

The task of the preacher

In the midst of a worshipping congregation of God's people, the original and proper function of the sermon is the preaching and teaching of the written Word of God. It is the unique privilege of the preacher on such an occasion to expound to the hearers the meaning of what God has to say in His Word, and to seek to apply truths thus discerned with some practical and pointed relevance to the circumstances, condition and opportunities of those present.

Every minister or pastor of a local church is indeed set apart before God to this very task – that he may give himself continually to prayer and to the ministry of the Word (see Acts 6:4). As a man able and expected to give time to study, as a man equipped with appropriate training and necessary books, as a man who continues to discipline his life with a view to proficiency in such ministry, he ought week by week to give to his congregation a continual increase of understanding in the revealed biblical truth. His hearers ought to be made continually aware that the Bible is his unfailing, sufficient and authoritative textbook, and that his supreme and sole concern is to set forth, not his own ideas, but the convictions of a faith plainly and explicitly grounded on God's written Word. He should discharge his stewardship as a man whose business it is to inform people of biblical teaching, and to cause them to understand how such truths concern both their daily lives and their eternal welfare.

To put the same truth in other words, those who preach to Christian congregations, or seek to make Christian truth known to non-Christians, ought always to be constrained by the recollection that the church is 'a witness and a keeper of Holy Writ' (The 39 Articles: Art. 20).

To quote Professor E. J. Bicknell on this point

> The church exists to propagate certain beliefs . . . Her message is sufficiently set forth in Scripture . . . Her primary function is that of witness . . . As a witness she cannot alter or add to the truth; she is the servant and not the mistress of her message. (*A Theological Introduction to The 39 Articles*, pp. 317f.)

In this connection, also, there is arresting and appropriate significance in the custom, common in some Reformed churches, that, before the minister enters the pulpit, the Bible should be carefully carried in and placed upon the rostrum, as a visible sign and freshly-acted witness that it is the one authoritative textbook that is reverenced and read in this congregation.

Much more than most of us are aware, such proper, full, expository, biblical preaching and teaching has become a forgotten practice and a lost art. The Bible is not faithfully and thoroughly expounded in our pulpits. Preachers practice 'imposition' not exposition. They choose so-called 'texts' as starting-points or pegs, from which to introduce, or on which to hang, what they have a mind to say. They do not properly acknowledge themselves – first in preparation and then during sermons – to be nothing but ministers or servants of God's Word, whose business it is solely to set forth for people's edification what can be got out of God's Word rather than what can be devised by the initiative of their own reasoning or imagination.

In consequence, with us 'a text' has come to mean something short, something which belongs to the preacher – *his* text – something which, because it is more or less just an indication of the subject, he can handle as he will. So he makes God's Word serve his ends instead of himself becoming a true servant of the Word of God. How far this is from the original and proper use of the word 'text' (as in the reference to the text of ancient manuscripts) where it describes simply the actual statements to be found in the Bible in any chosen passage, whether short or long. The business of the preacher is to stick to the passage chosen and to set forth exclusively what it has to say or to suggest, so that the ideas expressed and the principles enunciated during the course of the sermon plainly come out of the written Word of God, and have its authority for their support rather than just the opinion of their human expositor.

The task which requires doing is well described in Nehemiah 8:8: 'They read from the Book of the Law of God, making it clear [RSV has 'with interpretation'], and giving the meaning so that the people could understand what was being read.' People need to be made aware of the actual force and relevant truth of Bible passages. It is the preacher's privilege and duty to be such a steward of the mysteries of God, setting out plainly divinely-revealed truths. His responsibility both to God and to others is to be faithful in the discharge of this ministry, and to bring his hearers continually into the light, and under the judgment of the God-given Word.

The use of the whole Bible

We particularly need to recognize afresh that the preacher who would be truly faithful can adequately discharge his stewardship only if he preaches the whole Bible and the Christ of all the Scriptures. He ought, therefore, to make it plain, by the comprehensive variety of his themes, that his textbook is the whole Bible. In his practice he should show his belief that all Scripture, because it is 'given by inspiration of God', is profitable, and still intended of God to be useful for teaching, rebuking, correcting and training in righteousness (2 Tim. 3:16).

In his day this was stressed by John Calvin. Preaching on 2 Timothy 3:16,17 in a sermon entitled *The Proper Use of Scripture*, he said

> And that no man might take the liberty to choose what he pleaseth, and so obey God in part, St. Paul saith – the whole Scripture hath this majesty of which he speaketh, and that it is all profitable. To be short, St Paul informeth us that we must not pick and call the Scripture to please our own fancy, but must receive the whole without exception. Thus we see what St Paul's meaning is in this place, for when he speaketh of the Holy Scripture, he doth not mean that which he was then writing, neither that of the other apostles and evangelists, but the Old Testament. Thus we perceive that his mind was that the law and the prophets should always be preached in the church of Christ.

It is important, therefore, that every preacher should believe, and become increasingly aware in experience, that there is a vital Christian significance for present-day hearers to be found in Scriptures written long ago, and before Christ came. The Old Testament can and should mean more to us than it did or could during Old Testament times; for we live in the light and experience of their Christian fulfillment. Also the New Testament explicitly indicates that it was written for our instruction (see Rom. 15:4; 1 Cor. 10:11; 2 Tim. 3:15–17; cf. 1 Pet. 1:10–12). It has been divinely prepared and provided for our benefit, to help our understanding and enjoyment of salvation through faith in Christ.

For instance, 'St Paul (1 Cor. 10:11) says that the events of the Exodus happened to Israel (for example, Gk. *Tupikos*) by way of type'. 'For the exodus-theme (with its associated thoughts) provides the clue for the interpretation of each successive stage in God's redeeming acts.' 'The earlier story not only shows a correspondence with the later; it provides the imagery, the authoritative categories, by which alone the true meaning of the later can be understood' (W. Scott, 'The Christian Use of the Old Testament', *The Churchman* Vol. lxi, No. 4, p. 177.). Clearly, therefore, the Old Testament stories ought to be used and expounded as divinely-provided material for the better preaching and appreciation of Christ and the gospel.

In this connection, as C.H. Dodd has significantly shown, striking illustration of this method of exposition is to be found in the use of the Old Testament which is made by the New Testament writers. According to their judgment, the Holy Spirit speaks to us 'today' through the ancient Scriptures (see e.g. Heb. 3:7ff.). They appealed to the ancient scriptural history and statement to confirm the divine origin of, and to interpret the

divine purpose in, the events of the gospel or the experience of Christians. Paul therefore 'found a securer
basis than his own "experience" for the theology he
taught'.

> He expressly bases his theology upon the *kerygma* as illu-
> minated by the prophecies of the Old Testament; or, in
> other words, upon the historical facts which he had
> "received", from competent witnesses, set in the larger his-
> torical framework, witnessed, both as fact and as meaning,
> by the prophetic writers. (Dodd, *According to the Scriptures*,
> p. 135)

What is more important still, and finally decisive for all
His disciples, is that the first followers of Christ learnt
this method of understanding and of scriptural exposition from the risen Lord Himself. For, when He was talking to Cleopas and his companion on the road to
Emmaus, Jesus began 'with Moses and all the Prophets',
and 'explained to them what was said in all the
Scriptures concerning himself' (Luke 24:27).

Such appreciation of the place and need for the proper Christian use of the Old Testament in our pulpits is
the more urgently necessary because the literary and
historical criticism of the Old Testament, engaged in by
ministers in training more than by others, has developed
in the preachers-to-be of our churches a critical, 'scientific' attitude to the Old Testament documents, which
has actually inhibited rather than encouraged their use
of these Scriptures in the way in which a Christian
preacher should handle them. For 'the Bible has become
too much a book for specialists; a book on the serious
discussion of which men are hesitant to embark, lest
they trespass on some technical preserve, and be condemned out of hand for some highly technical errors'. 'It

is the great immediate loss produced by the historical study of the Bible that it has destroyed the old common believing use of the Bible.' (H. Cunliffe-Jones, *The Authority of the Biblical Revelation*, p. 35)

Preachers therefore, need to return to a proper Christian attitude to the Old Testament, and to a proper believing use of it in Christian preaching and teaching. What is more, to get to the root of the matter, those being trained as preachers in the theological colleges need to be set free from absorption in the study of the prevailing scientific and historical criticism of the Old Testament (which is for them not only so largely pointless but also so grievously deadening) and encouraged to study the Old Testament with its Christian application and use fully in view. For it is within the canon of the Old and New Testament Scriptures that God's present word for us is still to be found and heard. So the faithful steward of God-given revelation must preach the whole Scriptures and nothing but the Scriptures.

3

Relevant Bible Passages Expounded

Let's now consider three passages of Scripture which directly bear in their content on this subject of the God-given Word and its faithful ministry to us. In expounding them we have two objectives. First, our aim will be to discover what they have to teach. Second, we shall endeavour to show in a practical way how God's Word may in fact be expounded, so providing an illustration of a method which can be applied to other passages of Scripture.

a. The making of a prophet (1 Samuel 3:1–21)

NOTE: This example illustrates the decisive importance of expounding an incident in its context. What is recorded in this chapter is not simply the personal conversion of a child, but rather the call of a young man to be God's messenger to others.

EXPOSITION: The story of the call of the child Samuel is one with which most, if not all, of us have been familiar from childhood. But with most of us our intimate acquaintance with the chapter which contains the story ends at verse 10. It is, however, only from the latter part of the chapter that we discover fully why God called Samuel, and what it led to. For instance, in verse 20 we read, 'And all Israel from Dan to Beersheba recognized that Samuel was attested as a prophet of the LORD.' We do well, therefore, to study the chapter as a whole, particularly as we may learn from it, so to speak, how prophets and preachers are made; for we still need them. Let us then direct our attention to all the verses of 1 Samuel 3.

(i) *Why necessary.* At the beginning of the chapter we are told quite plainly why the making of a new prophet was necessary. We read that 'the word of the Lord was rare', or precious, 'in those days' (verse 1). In other words, men rarely heard a fresh and living message from God. There was a lack in the land of those who had the insight to see and the urge to declare the word of the Lord. The very language chosen to describe Eli perhaps suggests that he had become quite incapable of such a ministry; 'whose eyes were becoming so weak that he could barely see' (verse 2). There was danger, so to speak, that the very lamp of witness for God would go out, and that young and old would simply go to sleep, instead of being aroused and made to act by the challenge of God's word (verse 3). Then it was, at such a time as this, that the Lord Himself did something. He 'called Samuel' (verse 4).

Is there not a measure of parallelism in our present situation? Is there not some dearth in our land of preachers who speak as those who have received words from God which must be declared? Too many of those who have been trained to occupy our pulpits have been weakened, rather than established, in the conviction that in the Holy Scriptures there is still to be found the authoritative God-given Word for our generation. Do we not need afresh in our pulpits more men who can help people to hear God speak through His Word? Instead of having our churches served by 'priests', do not the people need afresh to be aroused by prophets and evangelists? Do we not need, ought we not to pray, that the Lord Himself would call some as He called Samuel, or as He called John Wesley, Charles Simeon, Spurgeon, and Moody to be mighty public preachers of the Word of God?

(ii) *How begun.* Let us see, then, how this making of a prophet was begun in Samuel's case. We are first given a description of his condition before it happened. There was a sense in which he was already in the ministry, or, as we might say, active in church work (see verse 1). Also, he was probably some years older than most pictures or stories based on this chapter suggest; for surely no young child can have been given by God such a message as the Lord gave to Samuel (see verses 11–14)? But 'Samuel did not yet know the LORD: The word of the LORD had not yet been revealed to him.' (verse 7). He had never met God alone and face to face. The Lord had never spoken direct to his heart. So he had no word to proclaim to men. This state of things was completely altered by three significant happenings, (a) The Lord called him personally and by name. (b) When at last he learnt how to answer the call and to make the proper response, God disclosed to him His word, (c) Although he was terrified to open his mouth, he was solemnly charged by Eli to declare what the Lord had said to him. For this word, which Samuel had been given, was clearly a word about others and for others; it was meant to be made known. So Eli warned Samuel very solemnly that he would bring judgment down upon his own head if he kept silent. When God selects a messenger and entrusts to him His word, God expects His message to be delivered. This is the compulsion that makes men preach – the awareness that they

have been given a word from God which must be pro-
claimed. (Compare Amos 3:7,8; 1 Cor. 9:16,17.)

(iii) *How furthered*. Samuel was helped by Eli to enter
into his calling. It is true that Eli was slow to appreciate
exactly what was happening in Samuel's experience.
But, in the end, he perceived that Samuel was being
called of God to the ministry of His word. What is more,
once Eli realized exactly what was happening, he gave
Samuel excellent advice, and the more excellent because
he kept himself out of any further necessary participation as a go-between. He told him to go back alone; and
wait on God to speak to him direct to reveal His word
and to disclose His mind. Still further, once Eli realized
what was happening, he was prepared to take God's
message from this young man and to submit to it,
though it spoke his own condemnation (verse 18). Such
a story makes one wonder about the state of things in
our own churches, whether some, who have grown old
in the ministry, are as quick as they ought to be to detect
that God is calling some young person in their congregation to the ministry of His Word; whether they are as
ready, once they have discerned this, to give helpful
spiritual guidance; whether, once the young adult
begins his ministry, they are as prepared to accept him as
God's messenger.

(iv) *How completed*. In the making of Samuel to be a
prophet it was the Lord Himself who completed what He
had begun. Samuel was fully established in his calling to
be a prophet of the Lord by a continuous experience of
meeting with God and receiving revelations through His
word which he preached to the people (verse 21, and
4:1a); and by the self-authenticating character of the message which he gave. The people were made unmistakably

aware that God was with Samuel, and that his messages were not from himself but from God; for God Himself confirmed and fulfilled them (verse 19). So 'all Israel . . . recognized that Samuel was attested as a prophet of the LORD' (verse 20). The word of God once again became a present living power in the land. They knew that there was a prophet in Israel. Let's hope that this divine pattern of prophet-making may be reproduced in our own congregations.

b. How to speak a word in season (Isaiah 1:4–11)

EXPOSITION: There is often no qualification more desirable in Christian ministry than the ability to speak the appropriate and helpful word to the spiritually needy and distressed. Such ability is acquired, on the one hand, by the gift of God, and, on the other hand, through the steadfast obedience of personal discipleship. Its acquisition is exemplified in the pattern Servant of the Lord, the incarnate Son of God Himself, prophetic witness to whose inner discipline and devotion is given in Isaiah 1. Christians who read verses 4 to 9 recognize that these words may be reverently regarded as uniquely true of Christ Himself. Here He discloses the secret of His inner life; God spoke to Him morning by morning. He declares His God-inspired readiness to do the Father's will. He unflinchingly faces suffering and reproach. He counts on God's sure help, and on His own triumphant vindication as God's Servant. We should find in this penetrating scriptural revelation a pattern for our own service and an indication of the conditions of effective ministry to others.

(i) *Be a daily listener and a docile learner* (1:4). 'The prophet', says George Adam Smith, 'learns his speech as the little child does by listening. Grace is poured upon the lips through the open ear.' While prophets of old often received divine disclosures in dreams or ecstatic visions of the night, this servant receives revelations when already wide awake. The Lord meets with him morning by morning, and teaches little by little what and how to speak to others. There is no equipment for the ministry comparable with this – to have the Lord to rouse one from sleep, to discover that He can awaken one's spirit as well as one's body to pay heed, and thus to be given private instruction alone with Him morning by morning.

(ii) *Be a devoted doer and a steadfast sufferer in the practice of obedience* (verses 5, 6). When we sit at the Lord's feet to learn of Him, we find that He gives not only the mind to understand, but also the will to obey. No matter how costly His demands, He can open our ears so that the spirit of rebellion and refusal is taken away. In its place there is given the spirit of devotion, even when the practice of obedience involves facing inevitable pain and persecution. Nor have the conditions of God's service in this world changed since Old Testament and New Testament times. Those who would be faithful in this ministry need to recognize clearly that such obedience, far from bringing earthly honour and advantage, is much more likely to bring suffering and reproach. What is demanded, therefore, is perseverance in unflinching consecration to the God-appointed pathway. Only those, who have themselves faithfully endured in this way, can be qualified to speak the encouraging word to others who have become weary and faint in mind (compare Heb. 12:3).

(iii) *Be a hopeful believer*, sure of God's active intervention and help (verses 7–9). For determination to endure is best inspired by strong confidence in God's certain aid. We need, therefore, to know and to prove that those who thus trust Him will never be disappointed and put to shame. Such a servant of God may well ask 'Who can condemn?' if it is God who justifies. Indeed, 'if God is for us, who can be against us?' (see Rom. 8:31–34). Such are the assurance and the outspoken assertion which can best bring new hope and courage to the depressed and the despondent. But no one can minister the inspiration of such hope to others, unless one has first made such confidence one's own, and proved its worth to strengthen steadfast endurance.

(iv) *Therefore become a decisive preacher, with a clear message of both hope and warning* (verses 10, 11). It is out of such discipline and devotion and dependence that the admired ability to speak the decisive word is born. Such a servant can gently exhort the despondent to trust in God and to take courage. To one whose heart is right (the one who 'fears the Lord'), to one whose feet are right (who 'obeys the word of his servant'), to one whose experience nevertheless seems all wrong (who 'walks in the dark, who has no light'), to all such in their tiredness and despondency this servant can say from the depth of his own experience of similar trials, 'Count on God's faithfulness. Trust in the name of the Lord. Stay upon your God'. Also, to any who try to provide themselves with artificial cheer ('Let's get drunk and have a laugh' they might say) and brighten their darkness with some temporary artificial light, the same servant gives the solemn warning that all such temporary relief will not finally help. Such hedonists will find, when the evening of life's passing enjoyment is over, that they must (to quote Matthew Henry) 'go to bed in the dark'.

Such then are the high privilege and solemn responsibility of the minister of the God-given Word – to bring challenge and warning to the self-confident and temporarily self-satisfied, in case they 'lie down in torment'; and to bring comfort and hope to the tired and discouraged, by encouraging them to trust in the name of the Lord, and to stay upon their God.

c. The practical value of the Holy Scriptures
(2 Timothy 3:14 – 4:2)

EXPOSITION: The sacred writings of the Bible are unique both in origin and purpose. Though men wrote them they are to be accepted as divinely-inspired. Just as the heavens (Ps. 33:6) and the human race (Gen. 2:7) were made by the breath of the Lord, so Scripture is to be regarded as 'God-breathed', the product of the creative activity of the divine Spirit. Writings so produced are said in every instance to be 'useful' (verse 16). They have a supreme practical value. This value God means us first to benefit from ourselves, and then to minister to others. None can come within its reach without being involved in responsibility for the use he makes of it. Let us consider what this passage, which speaks of the origin and purpose of the Scriptures, has to say about their practical value.

(i) *For salvation*. This is the first indispensable value of the Scriptures. They are able to make us 'wise unto salvation'. This implies that, until we discover what they have to offer us, we are both sinful and ignorant, needing both salvation and enlightenment. The Scriptures reveal that the benefit we need is to be found in Christ Jesus, through faith alone. This means that Jesus and His salvation – the Person and work of Christ – are the great central theme of the Scriptures. It also means that to enjoy the benefit offered we must fix our confidence not on the Book but on the Person, from whom the writings come, and of whom the writings speak. Further, because this Saviour is for all, and all need Him from their earliest days, the ideal way to learn of Him from the Bible is from one's youngest childhood, so that while still young one may trust in Him and find salvation.

(ii) *For education*. To become a child of God is a new beginning rather than an end. The believer in Christ Jesus is meant to progress to the full stature of Christian maturity and become 'of God'. This will only happen if one is willing to go to school with the Bible as textbook and the Spirit as Teacher. Adolescence is the period of life when we most need teaching, correction, and instruction.

Only those who are willing both to learn and to be corrected will advance to true adulthood. Here we need to realize that for this purpose all the Scriptures are profitable. It is possible, that is, to know only a small portion of the Bible, and yet to find Christ and to obtain salvation through faith in Him. So, in case we should be content to rejoice only in such Scriptures and to neglect the rest, we are here reminded that, because every Scripture is alike, 'God-breathed' (KJV), it is in every case capable of proving beneficial for our spiritual education. Therefore we ought to read and to pay attention to them all. We neglect them, or parts of them, at our danger and to our loss.

(iii) *For service*. When we have grown up to Christian adulthood, God's purpose is to use us to do His will and His work in the world. Such a career or course of action, such daily conduct, is possible only to those Christians who are adequately trained and equipped to face life in this way, and on every occasion to do that particular 'good work' which the circumstances demand, or for which they provide the golden opportunity. Such equipment is acquired only by those who are taught of God through the Scriptures, and have allowed their lives to be disciplined by the teaching of God's Word. Certainly none can share in the saving work of Christ, and go forth to do the supreme 'good work' of leading others to faith in Him, unless he knows the Scriptures, and how to use them in soul-saving work.

Notice, in conclusion, *our consequent responsibility* for their right use. Each individual Christian (see 3:14) who has been taught the Scriptures, and has been assured of their divine origin and supreme practical worth, has a direct personal responsibility to continue in these things – to walk in the light which he is privileged to enjoy. But furthermore, any who are called to the task of ministry to others (see 4:1,2) have a solemn public responsibility to be unfailingly faithful in preaching the Word on every occasion. No matter what kind of reception they get, it is for them to 'preach the word', to 'be prepared in season and out of season'; to 'correct, rebuke and encourage – with great patience and careful instruction'. In case they should be turned aside by the fear, or favour, or flattery, let them do such work as in the sight of God, and as those who must give account to Christ Jesus who shall judge the quick and the dead at His appearing.

So, because of the divine origin and supreme value of the Holy Scriptures, all who receive them ought to realize that they hold them in trust, and must give account of their stewardship. They demand of us the whole-hearted and increasing response both of personal obedience and of faithful ministry. We must then be diligent doers and persistent preachers of the Word, and not hearers or readers only.

4

Getting To Grips with the Task

1. Fundamental prerequisites

No one will expound the Bible as a Christian preacher and teacher ought unless he is primarily moved to it by a compelling sense of the supreme God-given authority of the Old Testament and New Testament Scriptures. Such a man must believe that he is called to handle and set forth the very oracles of God, the direct, decisive and final Word of divine revelation. He needs to realize that in a fallen, dark world, in a day of marked human despair, in a generation in which the feebleness of human effort are all too apparent, the one person who has something to offer worth having is the faithful Christian preacher; because he has to give to all the Word of God, which is the one thing that is stable, reliable and sure of fulfilment in a totally uncertain and insecure world.

The true biblical expositor needs also to be moved by a strongly established conviction concerning the significance of the biblical record and witness; a conviction which will make him give prominence to biblical themes, and resort freely and frequently to biblical illustrations. It will move him in his study and preparation to show an active and careful regard for the distinctive values in the expression of divine truth, which by God's providential overruling and direct inspiration are enshrined in biblical language and phraseology.

In addition, the indispensable condition of true satisfaction in biblical exposition is for the preacher consciously to become God's fellow-worker and with wonder and awe to realize in experience that God is pleased to use him to further His purposes in the lives of others. No preacher can enter into this satisfaction unless God's ends in the ministry of His Word become the preacher's own ends. His overriding and compelling concern must be to glorify God, to magnify Christ, to turn all from darkness to light, to lead them to acknowledge Christ as Saviour and Lord, in repentance and faith; and then to guide and encourage them regularly to find their place in the active worship and local fellowship of God's people, to follow after holiness, to do good works, to be Christ's witnesses in the world, and to rejoice in the hope of the glory of God and of the coming day of Christ.

His preaching should be both theological and inspirational, both doctrinal and devotional; evangelical in its primary witness and also ecclesiastical, ethical and eschatological in its complementary emphases. His concern should be from the whole Bible to declare the whole counsel of God and to make plain to his hearers that what they are asked to believe, and what as Christians they ought to practise, is all directly based on the explicit teaching of the written Word of God. He should produce by his instruction those who can support their faith and practice by appeal to the Bible, and who are themselves keen to learn from, to live by, and to make known, the revealed truth of God.

2. The selection of the text

In expository biblical preaching and teaching the selection of the particular text or passage of Scripture which is to be expounded is necessarily basic to all else. Both in private preparation and in public performance the faithful expositor must explicitly start with, and start from, one definite text or passage of Scripture, which he seriously intends to make it his business to examine and to expound.

Admittedly such a particular selection or opening announcement of the text to be specifically treated requires the true expositor to confine himself to this text. He must therefore seek, first in personal thought, reading and prayer, and then in his public preaching and teaching, to be the concentrated student and servant of this one passage. Such clearly defined limitation to a single text, which may at first seem unwelcome, has marked advantages both for preachers and hearers alike. The preacher has no longer to hunt everywhere for new ideas for his next sermon. He discovers them in his selected text by close-up investigation. For however similar their themes may sometimes be, different passages of Scripture all vary in the manner of their presentation of these themes. So the preacher who discovers and develops the distinctive ideas and emphases of each different text will find his sermons made fresh and different by the very demands of detailed exposition.

Hearers, too, will be made aware by his textual exposition that the preacher is making them see what the Bible itself says, and getting his thoughts from the written Word. This will give to his hearers deep, enduring enrichment of the kind that will come home to them with divine rather than merely human authority – the authority, that is, of the inspired Word of God. The preacher may depart or be forgotten, but his texts they will meet again. Because of his faithful exposition of their significance, they will hear or read them with added insight, and feel their force and inspiration at a deeper level.

Again, those who learn from such an expository preacher how to obtain from the Scripture fresh insight and inspiration will thereby be encouraged to use the Bible with more diligence and devotion in their private lives. The preacher's example may influence them to read it for themselves with increased faith, zeal and satisfaction, because they have experienced, under the preacher's ministry, how God can use the written Word and its careful and prayerful study to give light and understanding, encouragement and hope.

3. The necessary concentration

The ministry to others of true biblical exposition is costly and exacting in its demands. This is one reason why so few fully undertake it. It requires nothing less than the sincere consecration of the whole man and the sustained concentration of his undivided and undistracted mind. The would-be expository preacher must give time and give himself to the necessary preparatory study of God's written Word. The only way for a man fully to get hold of a passage, or to get into a passage, is for him to dwell on it long enough for it to get a deep hold on him, and a deep entrance into his being. This involves toil and sweat, thought and prayer, faith and good works, patience and perseverance.

F.B. Meyer wrote

> Expository preaching is the consecutive treatment of some book or extended portion of Scripture on which the preacher

has concentrated head and heart, brain and brawn, over which he has thought and wept and prayed until it has yielded up its inner secret, and the spirit of it has passed into his spirit. The highest point of sermon utterance is when a preacher is 'possessed', and certainly in the judgment of the writer such possession comes oftenest and easiest to a man who has lived, slept, walked and eaten in fellowship with a passage for the best part of a week.

In order to get the best ultimate results in such preaching it is, therefore, desirable in preparation to return at intervals several times to the same passage, with the determination, every time one reconsiders it, to get a fuller hold of it, or to see something fresh in it. This method will also, at the same time, secure the stimulation and co-operation of the subconscious mind. For, once it is thus made aware that there is a job of comprehension and re-expression – of intake and output – to be done, the subconscious mind will, during the intervals between conscious study, make its own contributions towards the desired achievement of the full mental digestion and clear verbal exposition of the passage under consideration.

Since many would-be preachers never properly submit themselves to this discipline it is important to emphasize its necessary place. To repeat, therefore; one must make deliberate, concentrated, sustained, varied, frequently renewed attempts fully to understand the meaning of the text which is to be expounded. One must aim so to grasp the sense that one can, and sometimes actually will, express the sense in writing in one's own words.

One may compare the task of translating into English a previously 'unseen' passage from a foreign language. Before you can make complete sense of the details, it is important to become aware of the theme and of the run of the passage as a whole, to grasp its literary character, its main ideas, its sequence of thought. So one should aim clearly to 'see the wood' before puzzling too closely about the identity and the contribution of particular 'trees'. The preacher, therefore, should get a comprehensive view of the whole before deciding on the significance of particular details, or supposing that he can adequately treat the passage under three slick and rather quickly (if cleverly) devised subheadings. Otherwise he may become more interested in developing his own subheadings than in faithfully drawing out the full content and significance of the text.

Next, once the main theme and thread of the passage have become meaningful, one should move closer to the text, and examine details, as under a microscope, point by point, phrase by phrase, even word by word.

In all such investigation it is of major importance to seek accurately to identify what is there. If he is genuinely to bring ideas out of the text, and not to read his own ideas or preferences into it, the preacher must be properly objective, and not secretly, or even unconsciously, more than half-subjective in his appreciation. In all such investigations it is of fundamental importance to seek to grasp both the grammar and the history of the Bible passage. It goes without saying that where possible the passage should be studied in the original Greek or Hebrew. But in any case, whether he knows these languages or not, the preacher should welcome and use modern translations and paraphrases, and any other aids which bring him nearer to an exact understanding of the original text. It is helpful, also, to add to one's own understanding, and particularly to stimulate one's own thinking, by reading what others have to say in explanation of the text. There is great value in Bible commentaries. But they should, however, be kept subordinate and subservient to the understanding of the text itself; and one should aim all the time ultimately to get beyond them and to reach an independent appreciation and expression of the thought and significance of the passage.

This writer can testify that, if one thus saturates the mind with a passage, and gives it time and opportunity to dissolve under one's meditation, the mind will hold it, so to speak, in solution. One can then ultimately reach the point where the absorbed ideas – the more so as they are warmed by believing prayer – will crystallize out and produce a solid deposit, something substantial yielded by the passage and suitable to set forth in exposition to others. The actual experience of this happening establishes one in the confidence that it can happen again; thus it becomes a goal worthy of our diligent pursuit.

Finally, such achievement is supremely satisfying. For to be allowed and enabled to think God's thoughts after Him in this way, and to gain fresh insight into His mind and ways, is the highest kind of discovery. In addition, to such discovery is joined the delight as well as the duty of sharing it with others. Biblical exposition admittedly cannot be worthily undertaken without much hard work. But those who do it find also that it is never truly done without thrill and satisfaction. For these are its unfailing rewards: first, for oneself, to comprehend and to appreciate the divine mind in the divine Word; and then, to embody and express one's understanding of it in one's own words so that others can enjoy it, and be enriched by it. Privileged and doubly blessed is the man whom God calls to such a ministry.

4. Definition of the theme and of the aim

If the ultimate public exposition of a passage or text from the Bible is to have the character of a real sermon, in contrast to the discursive comment of a so-called Bible reading, it is necessary that the treatment should be given both unity and practical application. In other words, the intending preacher must develop his expository treatment of the text in relation to a single dominant theme, and in its presentation must concentrate on the realization of a corresponding practical aim in his instruction and exhortation of his hearers. It is the lack of such careful selective 'finish' in the preparation and presentation of the exposition that understandably makes some hearers feel that expository methods in the pulpit can be rambling, indefinite and unending, and tend to lack the clear instruction and the pointed challenge of more topical sermons.

The would-be expository preacher, therefore, must not only undertake the preparatory work already indicated as necessary, but must at the same time seek to discern what is – for the occasion of ministry which he has in mind – the main thrust or obvious message from God in the passage at which he is working. Some passages are very fertile. They are capable of a number of selective treatments according to the points in them chosen for emphasis and according to the corresponding particular aim and application which the preacher may have in view. What is important is that the preacher should decide on one definite subject or emphasis for each particular occasion of ministry, and should then use from the material and ideas which he has acquired by his working at the text only those which are obviously related to this subject. In a sermon, as distinct from a running commentary, reference to points irrelevant to the chosen subject must ruthlessly be omitted. By such discipline the preacher can give to his treatment of the passage not only a desirable brevity and coherence, but also a significant development and drive wholly in the one chosen direction, which should be the direction of his intended aim and his proposed closing application.

How such ideas actually work out in practice is best indicated by illustrative treatment of a particular passage. Here a so-called fertile passage is deliberately chosen in order to show how much variety of use may sometimes be possible. Also, difference in treatment and in application should in measure be influenced by the character of the hearers to whom one has to minister. For each treatment of a passage of any length, such as a narrative or a parable, it is helpful, where that proves possible, to take a limited brief quotation as a kind of short 'text' or suggestive pithy thought.

Illustrative treatments of John 2:1–11

a. At a wedding

Short text: 'Jesus . . . had also been invited to the wedding' (verse 2).

Aim: To suggest that Jesus should be invited into married life: and why.

Introduction: Have you thought of inviting Jesus to your wedding?

Main content: (i) The difference the presence of Jesus can make. He did not 'kill joy', or increase difficulty. He helped when natural resources failed. He gave them something better to enjoy. (ii) The underlying conditions of realized benefit. Inviting Jesus to come. Going to Him when difficulties arise, i.e. prayer. Doing what He says, i.e. obedience.

At a women's meeting

Short text: 'They have no more wine' (verse 3).

Aim: To suggest what Christ can do in the home: and how.

Introduction: Problems of housekeeping: money not enough: inviting extra and unexpected visitors causes shortage.

Main content: (i) How problems in the home can be resolved. Take them, like Mary did, to Jesus: i.e. take it to the Lord in prayer. Do what He demands and directs: act according to His word. N.B. – This may involve having to do what seems no use, e.g. filling water pots with water, when the need is wine. (ii) The twofold result. Not only is something better than before experienced (i.e. 'the good wine'), but also such a home becomes a witness for God, where Christ is magnified, and individuals learn to believe in Him.

At a meeting for prayer

Short text: verse 3 in full.

Aim: To indicate features essential to effectual prayer.

Introduction: In this story we see a need met, and a situation transformed, because someone took the need to Christ.

Main content: What effectual prayer involves: (i) Going to Jesus about it. Going not only in self-interest, but also with active concern for the needs of others. (ii) Acknowledging His power: expecting Him to be able to do what we cannot. Acknowledging His wisdom and love: i.e. giving up (like Mary did) our own ideas of how, and acknowledging that His way is best (see verse 5). (iii) Being ready to act in obedience to His word: such obedience may be essential to the outworking of the divine answer.

An address to (potential) workers for Christ

Short text: 'Do whatever he tells you.' (verse 5).

Aim: To show how one may be used in Christ's service.

Main content: (i) The Requisites. Concern for the need of others. Going to Christ in believing prayer. Readiness to obey; to accept and do what He directs, not what we think. Willingness to be tested in private before being used in public, and possibly to put personal shortcomings right first. (Maybe it was the servants' job to fill the water pots, and they had not done it.) Readiness to make the venture of faith, counting on divine co-operation. (ii) The Results. The Lord's power manifested. He works as we act. We become fellow-workers with Him. The result is clearly His doing, not ours. Men's needs are met and they enjoy something far better than before – a new creation. Our own knowledge of the Lord and our personal faith in Him are increased.

Preaching to a local congregation

Short text: 'The master of the banquet . . . did not realize where it had come from, though the servants who had drawn the water knew' (verse 9).

Aim: To awaken some to an appreciation of their Christian heritage.

Introduction: The good things which we enjoy we easily take for granted. We tend to suppose they are produced as a matter of course. We may even wonder why some are not produced sooner (see 5:10).

Main content: Need to realize that the best is only available because of the following. Someone has had eyes to see need, and a heart to care about it. Someone has prayed. Someone has responded to the demands and the discipline of the obedience of faith. The Lord Himself has wrought His miracle of new creation.

At an evangelistic service

Short text: This, the first of his miraculous signs, Jesus performed in Cana in Galilee. He thus revealed his glory, and his disciples put their faith in him. (verse 11).

Aim: To awaken appreciation of, and response to, Christ.

Main content: Truths to which 'the good wine' bears witness. (i) Concerning Christ's Person or identity: who He is. He is the One who makes all things new. He has the power of God to create. This 'sign' was a manifestation of His unique glory. (ii) Concerning the character of Christ's work. To bring blessing to us – not judgment.

Contrast first plague (Ex. 7:17–21) – water turned to blood so that they could not drink. To give us something better than they have naturally in this first creation: and to give them the best at the end, when the natural fails. (Cf. 1 Cor. 15:46,49–54; 2 Cor. 4:16 – 5:2.) To give us something better than law-keeping and religious ceremonies could afford. The water-pots stood for formal superficial purification; the wine signified inner heart satisfaction, the blessing of new creation. (Cf. John 1:17; Heb. 7:15–19, 9:9,13,14.)

Conclusion: The direct personal challenge of His manifestation. To acknowledge His Person. To believe in Him. To enjoy the benefits of His revealed purpose and power.

An additional full-length exposition of this same passage is to be found in chapter 5.

5

Expounding Narrative

There are three main types of biblical subject-matter which may be treated in an expository manner. These are (i) narratives, (ii) short significant statements and (iii) longer reasoned or literary passages. In the following chapters we shall deal with each of these in turn. The easiest to begin with are Bible stories, whether historical narrative, particularly gospel incidents, or parables. Here the very nature of the subject-matter compels one to treat several or even many verses as a single unit, and therefore as one's real 'text'.

All preachers ought frequently to recollect that the Bible as a whole is largely a history or story book. It is full of the concrete. It is not so much a textbook of rules and of abstract principles as a collection of examples or typical cases. In its study truths are learnt and illustrated from their occurrence in actual life. God makes Himself and His will known to men and women by action or demonstration. His ways and His work complement, indeed they are themselves, His word to us; though they unquestionably need both the reliable record and the inspired interpretation of the written Word to make their witness to others fully permanent and significant.

This divinely-appointed place and purpose of stories in the Bible needs to be recognized as a guide to their right use. Such stories are written not just for our entertainment, but for our spiritual enlightenment, education and encouragement; and also, in some cases, for our admonition, reproof and correction (Rom. 15:4; 1 Cor. 10:6,11; 2 Tim. 3:16). Some of them are 'signs' divinely-intended to help us to acknowledge Christ, and to find life through faith in His Name (see John 20:30,31). The stories of the Bible are said, therefore, to provide 'examples' or 'types'; they are the very language of revelation. From them we may learn first, the ways of God, and second, God's ways for his children; in other words, we may learn what to believe about God's actions, and how to behave in the ordering of our own. This means that, rightly interpreted and applied, they can afford practical guidance in worthy and worthwhile living.

In evaluating what particular stories have to teach, it is important to discover, and to concentrate on, the main point – the one obvious spiritual truth or moral principle which each story illustrates. Some interpretation of Scripture which is purely allegorical can appear very arbitrary and fanciful. Our exposition will have more obvious force and appeal if it leads to the direct appreciation of the story's moral significance, whether the application concerns God's character and conduct or ours. For instance, in the interpretation of the parable of the Good Samaritan there have been those who have wished to regard the inn, the innkeeper and the two pence as signifying the church, the minister and the two sacraments, provided by God for the care of those saved from sin. Such suggestions scarcely carry full conviction. In the interpretation of this part of the story, if significance is to be discerned, it seems more reasonable and realistic to find indication of the need of after-care or follow-up work. It is not enough to rescue the destitute. For their further care and complete restoration or salvation the help of a more permanent institution or fellowship is necessary. In the discharge of such ministries those who cannot help by direct service may co-operate by bearing the expense.

In more detailed illustration of methods of treatment we now offer extended exposition of several passages. Distinctive features of some of these examples are also indicated in explanatory notes.

a. The way of healing (Exodus 15:23–26)

NOTE: The tree here cast into the bitter waters to make them sweet has often been said to point to the cross of Christ – the tree on which He bore our sins, that by His stripes we might be healed (1 Peter 2:24). Do we not rightly sing of the cross of Christ, 'It sweetens every bitter cup'? But however evangelical, however true to Christ and the gospel, however ultimately desirable, this may seem, to jump to such an interpretation – without apparent reason – is possibly unjustified, the sign of prejudice! Such a reaction is quite understandable.

It is possible to suggest a more reasonable and realistic approach to the same goal, an approach grounded on an explicit exposition of what the passage teaches. For this story bears witness to God's anticipating providence. God had already provided the remedy. The necessary 'tree' was already there alongside the need, waiting to be discovered and used. This is evidence of a truth about God's handiwork. It provides encouragement to research scientists to expect to find in God's creation remedies and cures for all nature's ills. It is also evidence that, when the way of healing is discovered and used, God Himself ought to be acknowledged as the prescribing Physician and the true Healer. (See verse 26: 'I am the LORD, who heals you'.) So-called human 'inventions' or 'discoveries' are, in the original sense of the word 'invention', only things which we 'come upon' or 'find' already there, having been put there for such use by the all-wise Creator. This awareness of God's ways rightly leads on to the expectation, and then to the discovery, that for our greatest malady – that of sin – God planned and provided a remedy before the foundation of the world in the Lamb to be slain. So we can use this passage to point to the atoning sacrifice of incarnate God. Nor do we have to invent a new gospel. We have only to discover the gospel already divinely provided. But this we shall not do apart from divine guidance and illumination. It was the Lord who showed Moses the tree.

EXPOSITION: (i) *Trials of the Christian pilgrimage.* 'When they came to Marah, they could not drink its water because it was bitter' (verse 23). This happened to God's people, after their redemption from Egypt, when He was leading them on their journey to the promised land. So we may rightly regard the incident as a picture not only of the trials of life, but more particularly of the trials of our Christian pilgrimage. The question of fundamental importance, therefore, is what was the attitude of God's people to such a trial? and what is our attitude today?

It is doubtless natural to regard such trials with surprise. So Jesus warned His disciples to make no mistakes in their thinking; 'in the world you will have trouble' (John 16:33). Similarly, the apostle Peter wrote, 'do not be surprised at the painful trial you are suffering, as though something strange were happening to you' (1 Pet. 4:12). For the experience of trial is clearly God's appointed road for His children. He has a purpose in it.

(ii) *Murmuring – or prayer*? If God's people are not sure of His purposeful providence there is very real danger that such trials become an offence. This happened to the Israelites. They murmured or complained; they resented and disbelieved; they even said Egypt would be better, and talked of going back – that is, we have here the beginnings of apostasy. No wonder the Holy Ghost still says, 'Today, if you hear his voice, do not harden your hearts' (see Heb. 3:7–13). On the other hand, Moses 'cried out to the Lord' (verse 25). His action indicates that such trial presented an opportunity for believing prayer, for expecting God to work. Nor was such confidence misplaced. If God had redeemed them from Egypt, if God intended to bring them in to the promised land, surely He could be trusted to see them through the intervening wilderness? So, in similar circumstances, we too can sing,

> He cannot have taught us to trust in His Name,
> And thus far have brought us to put us to shame.
> The tried soul trusts and prays, not doubts and murmurs.

(iii) *The answer of God*. Moses' faith was rewarded and his prayer answered. There were three steps which led to the solution of the trial. First, *divine provision*. The Lord showed Moses a tree, and said, in effect, 'That is the answer. I have long ago put it there for this very purpose, to meet this very need.' Second, *divine revelation*. The Lord showed him the tree. Moses was quite unaware that the answer was already provided and available, just waiting to be used, until God opened his eyes. Third, *human appropriation*. Moses cast the tree into the waters. By an act of responsive faith and practical obedience Moses applied the remedy, and enjoyed the benefit; the waters were made sweet.

(iv) *The deeper significance of the experience* was now perceived and commented on. Obviously God made it plain to them, and it is written for our learning.

1. 'There he tested them.' God's declared purpose in the trial was to test their heart response, to see whether they would murmur, or whether they would offer the prayer of faith and make the response of obedience. Compare Deuteronomy 8:2. So God still allows His people to encounter trials in order to discover whether we have a trustful heart or a resentful and unbelieving spirit.

2. 'There the LORD made a decree and a law for them.' The experience disclosed and confirmed God's appointed method of dealing with His people. It gave them opportunity to prove Him and His faithfulness. They were, in consequence, meant more permanently to learn that God answers in a threefold way the trials of His people. First He does so by an anticipating providence. God, who foresees every trouble long before it actually occurs, commonly provides against it beforehand. This is true naturally, as is strikingly evidenced by the discovery of medicinal remedies for physical diseases. It is true most of all spiritually. Our greatest ill, the malady of sin, God provided against long ago, by the Lamb slaughtered, so to speak, before the foundation of the world. Secondly, He does so by answering prayer, and making His provision known to the seeking soul. Our full discovery of such divine provision depends upon divine revelation. When we pray we realize that before we have called God has answered. So the revealing Spirit shows to the sin-stained for their healing the already finished work of Christ, the tree on which He bore our sin in His own body. Thirdly, God

assists His people in their trials by healing those who act in obedience. This is the way of healing, to trust and to obey. Those who diligently hearken to His voice and keep all His statutes may know God for themselves in their own experience as the Lord who heals.

(v) *The practical challenge.* This incident makes plain that in our lives the need and God's remedy can exist alongside each other, and yet never as yet have been brought together. For some have never seen what is God's remedy; and others, who have been shown, have so far failed to act. Discovery and enjoyment of God's remedy await first the prayer, and then the obedience, of faith. Before we pray, God provides; He has provided. When we pray the Lord directs and discloses; we see His answer. As we obey the Lord heals or works to bless.

b. The manifestation of Christ's glory (John 2:1–11)

NOTE: Here the evangelist himself explicitly comments on the significance of this event. He says it marked the beginning of Jesus' use of signs; and that, as a sign, it was a manifestation of Christ's glory, which led those who were responsive to His teaching (i.e. 'disciples') to faith in His Person. If, therefore, the passage as a whole is to be fully expounded, and its chief witness to the truth of God used and enforced, this obviously is the subject to be treated. Note that this emphasis is determined not by the preacher's preference, but by the direct indication of the Scripture itself. (Note also that in the Church of England Prayer Book this passage is appointed to be read on the Second Sunday after Epiphany.)

EXPOSITION: Epiphany means manifestation. Christ's glory was specially manifested by the first miracle

which He wrought in Cana of Galilee. In his record of
the incident the evangelist John calls it the first of
Christ's signs (see verse 11). For to some who were there
it meant very much more than the enjoyment of fresh
wine. True, the guests at the wedding did get their material need supplied; but some who were there had their
eyes opened to something far more wonderful. They
made a spiritual discovery. They saw Christ's glory.
They became aware of the unique wonder of His Person.
They believed in Him.

There are, therefore, two views of this incident: one is
what the ordinary guests at the wedding saw; the other
is what the disciples of Jesus saw. This difference of
understanding and insight is explicitly noted in the
course of the narrative. The ruler of the feast, we are
told, tasted the wine and appreciated its excellence; but
there was something which he did not know. He had no
idea how it had been produced. But the servants who
brought it in knew. This kind of deeper knowledge is
what we may well want as we meditate upon this passage, that we, too, may discern the manifestation of
Christ's glory, and with fresh conviction and renewed
purpose may believe in Him; that we also may see that
such miracles are only wrought first by the presence and
creative power of Christ, and then when others come
into personal relation and active co-operation with Him.
Briefly there were, and commonly still are, three conditions of the manifestation of His glory.

(i) *Believing prayer*. First, humanly speaking, the miracle
only happened because someone had eyes for the needs
of others and faith to believe that Jesus could meet the
need. So Mary went to Him and said, 'They have no
wine.' It is obvious from His answer to her that she
believed not only that He could do something, but also

that such an occasion provided opportunity for the open manifestation of Himself. While He did not disappoint the first confidence, He told her plainly that His hour for the full realization of the second hope was not yet come. At this gentle but firm rebuke Mary's faith rose still higher. For, instead of taking offence, she gave up her own ideas, and as one wholly prepared to trust not only His power to help, but also His wisdom and love to do the best, she said to the servants who were standing by awaiting instructions, 'Do whatever he tells you'; or, in other words, 'Do not look to me and my ideas; but look to Him, and act at once on His command'.

(ii) *Obedient faith*. In the second place the miracle happened as these servants responded to the commands of Christ and co-operated with Him. Their faith had first to be disciplined. The Lord tested them in private to see whether they would obey, before He used them in public to minister to others. For He wanted absolute unquestioning obedience to His word, the obedience of men who did not necessarily understand why, but who knew whom they had believed. He wanted obedience to His word just because it was *His* word. So He asked them to fill the water pots with water. This must have seemed to have no connection with the need of the moment. But they did not ask, 'Why?' They obeyed; and filled them up to the brim. Then, as to men who could now be counted on to make the supreme venture of obedience counting only and absolutely on His word, He told them to draw the water, and to carry it to the tables where the guests were feasting. They obeyed; and as they went, the Lord of creation became their fellow-worker. For He is faithful; when we count on His promise and obey His word, He fulfils it. This is how the miracles of ministry to our spiritual needs are still fulfilled, in the pathway of faith's obedience.

(iii) *Creative power*. In the third place the miracle was wrought by the present Lord. To begin with He was there – by personal invitation. Then He had been acknowledged as able – by seeking and responsive faith. So, finally, He acted to give practical expression to His unique divine power – the power to create – and thus to *manifest His glory*. For the governor of the feast was wrong. He expressed surprise that the best wine had been kept to the end. But it had not been kept. Only a few minutes before it was non-existent. It was a new creation. This is the hallmark of the activity of God, the sign that the Lord Jehovah Himself is at work – that the new takes the place of the old. Isaiah spoke of it in terms of the fir tree replacing the thorn (see Is. 55:13). Jesus gave concrete illustration of it in terms of the water being made into wine. Those who have their eyes opened to see in this the manifestation of Christ's distinctive glory become those who believe in Him, that He will do for them what He did for the water. So can sinners become new creatures in Christ Jesus (see 2 Cor. 5:17), a transformation which is but the 'beginning' of a life-long experience of His wonder-working power. So may we be 'to the praise of his glorious grace' (Eph. 1:6), as we trust Him both in us and through us to 'reveal his glory'.

(Alternative outline treatments of this passage are provided on pages 100 to 104).

c. The way and the call to win others for God (Luke 5:1–11)

NOTE: Here the various features of the narrative acquire greater potential significance if the whole record is treated as unified, and if the ultimate aim of Christ is regarded as determining in some measure every detail of His activity from the beginning of His contact with the fishermen. This aim (see verses 10 and 11) clearly was to call some particular men to leave their present occupation of catching fish, and to share in His work of winning souls. This means, therefore, that in principle our Lord Himself is here seen doing what He desired to invite the fishermen to do. So in this way we are made aware not only of the job to be done, but also of the way to do it.

EXPOSITION: In studying Christ's dealings with the men who became His chosen disciples and apostles we may learn two things: first, what His purpose was for them; and second, how He brought them to respond to this. Applying this to ourselves it means that, in studying this subject, we may learn what is the work Christ most wants us to do, and also, from His example, how we should do it. What He always wants to do is to reach our neighbours, to save them from self, to win their allegiance to Himself, and then to use them to reach others. So, when He called Simon and Andrew He said, 'Come, follow me, and I will make you fishers of men' (Mark 1:17). And the record given by Luke reveals in significant detail how He brought them to the point where they made the response He desired in order to produce the result He intended. Two things, therefore, here confront us. We have an illustration from the Master Workman of the way in which to reach others, and also His own call to us to follow Him and share in doing the same work. Let's seek then from His example to learn how to do it.

(i) *Jesus came where they were.* He came into their world, to the lakeside, to the boat and the nets. This is a principle of the gospel, of the incarnation and the cross – to come down where men and women are. This also is a principle of good teaching – to start from the known in order to proceed to the unknown. So Christ began here, by speaking to them first about their boat.

(ii) *He tested their attitude to Himself.* He did this indirectly and very simply, by asking them to let Him use their boat. When they consented they revealed, not only that they were friendly towards Him, but also that they were willing to be publicly associated with Him and His preaching work. Note, too, that in teaching it is often helpful to begin by asking one or two questions, the answers to which will reveal where your hearers stand, and how far they have already got in relation to the subject.

(iii) *He gave them something practical and instructive to do.* Christ asked them to show their attitude by action. When He thus used their boat He was giving them an object lesson in preparation for its deeper application later. For they discovered, doubtless to their surprise, that Jesus could take something of theirs and use it in an entirely new way. He turned the boat into a pulpit. The boat, which they had always used to catch fish for self, He used to reach men and women for God. Such was the result of surrendering it to Him.

(iv) *He tested their willingness to let Him help them.* He offered to help them catch fish. They might have been too proud, or too unbelieving, to receive His help. Many are. They might have wondered on the human level what He, a carpenter from the hills, could teach them about fishing. Surely they knew all there was to know about fishing. But our Lord's offer was skilfully chosen and well timed. They had worked all night and taken nothing. They could not deny their failure. The question was, would they act on His word?

(v) *He proved their faith, and let them prove His faithfulness, in their own familiar world of fishing.* Christ did not simply ask for verbal assent. He gave them something to do, and to do openly before their onlooking fellow fishermen. Their response was a further expression of their attitude to Him. They counted completely on His word and His faithfulness. Nor were they disappointed or put to shame. This is the kind of relationship to Him and His Word that issues in real progress, the relationship that touches our need, promises His help, demands our action, and gives us practical experience of His power.

(vi) *Simon discovered the fuller truth both about Jesus and about himself.* The miraculous draught of fishes brought other things to light. First, it revealed the Person of Jesus as no ordinary man, but the Lord. Second, and inevitably, this made Simon aware of his personal unfitness for such company. Deeper acknowledgment of Christ and painful conviction of sin both came to the birth. 'Go away from me, Lord; I am a sinful man!'

(vii) *The Lord revealed the amazing wonder of His saving grace and of His transforming power.* For when Simon told Him to depart, Jesus did not depart. He never does when with shame we confess our sin. For He came to save sinners; and it is the penitent and contrite whom He receives. What is more, to Simon Jesus offered the prospect of an entirely new life. 'Don't be afraid; from now on you will catch men.' For He can change sinners into soul-winners. What He had done for their fishing and their boat, He now offered to do for the fishermen themselves, to turn failure into success, and to use them to reach men. The Christ who turned a boat into a pulpit now began to make fishermen into preachers.

(viii) *They gave themselves to a new Master and a new business*. Such compelling constraint they could not deny. They gave up everything and followed Him. Before this they had spent their days just getting for self. From this point on they were to find life in giving themselves to Him and in 'catching' others for God. The Master's business became their God-given calling. Is it yours?

d. Answering the expectation of the needy (Mark 9:14–29)

NOTE: In the exposition of this passage illustration is briefly afforded of the seven constituent parts of full homiletical treatment. (For an able and exhaustive study in such analysis of sermon construction see *The Theory of Preaching* by Austin Phelps, first published by Scribner's, New York, 1881.) These seven parts are:

(i) *The Text* or passage to be expounded,

(ii) The Explanation, i.e. brief comment on the text to indicate its context and content.

(iii) *The Introduction*. This term is here used in a particular way, not simply to refer to the introduction of the hearers to the subject, which has here been largely begun already by the *Explanation*, but rather to refer to the introduction of the subject to the hearers. This should arrestingly indicate the practical relevance of the subject to the hearers, and suggest reasons why they certainly will, or ought to, be interested in its exposition,

(iv) *The Proposition*. This states in the briefest and clearest form the subject of the exposition which is to follow.

(v) *The Divisions*. These break up the proposed treatment into main sections with appropriate subheadings.

(vi) *The Development*. This fills in this outline framework, and possibly introduces further subdivision. Such subdivision should, however, be kept clearly subordinate, and not given such prominence that the hearers are confused by too many subheadings.

(vii) *The Conclusion*. This possibly makes a final brief survey or summary of the ground covered. It certainly should make a pointed application of the theme to the hearers, challenging them to some appropriate responsive action.

EXPOSITION:

(i) *The Text*. Mark 9:14–29: especially verse 18b: 'I asked your disciples to drive out the spirit, but they could not.'

(ii) *The Explanation*. Here is the scene at the foot of the mountain to which Jesus descended immediately after His transfiguration. When He arrived He found His disciples surrounded by a curious crowd, questioning scribes, and a man in need. The man immediately reproached Jesus with His disciples' failure. 'Here am I in great trouble and need', he said. 'I asked your disciples to do something to help. They have failed me.'

(iii) *The Introduction*. Such an incident immediately suggests a question which concerns us. What today, in the place where we are, is the attitude of the onlooking world to us as professed Christians? What do they think of us? Still more, what is the attitude of the needy, who perhaps have looked to us for help, and have been disappointed? How can we as Christ's disciples face up to the demands of those in need, and bring glory to our Master?

(iv) *The Proposition*. Let us therefore use our study of this passage to seek to appreciate how Christians should help people who are in need. We may entitle our study: '*Answering the expectation of the needy*'.

(v) *The Divisions*. We will concentrate our interest on three main points: first, the attitude of the man in need; second, how the man's need was met; and third, how disciples of Christ may share in such ministry.

(vi) *The Development*.

1. *The attitude of the man in need*. First, *he expected something of Christ's disciples*. This is a very noteworthy fact; and one that is still true. If we profess to be Christians, at once the onlooking world expects of us a different standard of behaviour. The person in need looks to us for help. People wait and watch with critical or with hopeful eye to see whether we can rise to the challenge. This is in itself a witness from outside that Christianity does stand for something in the world. Second, *he expected Christ's disciples to be able to relieve his distress*. This is still more remarkable. People expect Christians not only to be different, to act differently, but also to be able to do things for others, to come to the rescue. Such still are the challenge and the opportunity associated with being Christ's disciple. Third, *he was disappointed: and so became doubtful concerning even Christ's power to help*. He spoke to Jesus in an uncertain and questioning way. 'If you can do any thing,' he said, 'take pity on us and help us.' This

means that the disciples' failure undermined and weakened such faith as the man did have, when he first came, in Christ Himself.

2. *How the man's need was met.* First, *it was met because Jesus came.* He is the one and only answer to human need. Apart from Him, His coming and His working, we all must fail. Also the marvel of His coming to us in our need is here illustrated. Jesus chose to leave the glory of heaven on the mountain to face the suffering and need of the valley. When His three disciples wanted to stay to enjoy the bliss, when Jesus Himself had every right to depart to heaven in glory, He came down to face suffering and sacrifice, in order to minister to the needy. Second, *it was met because Jesus can.* Once He arrived there was no more uncertainty. Jesus swept aside the man's questioning. '"If you can"?', He asked. 'Everything is possible for him who believes.' The only thing still necessary was true human response, genuine simple faith. Then the man threw himself upon the Saviour's mercy and power; and the deed was done.

3. *How disciples may share in such ministry.* There is a third point to be noted. It comes in the story chiefly as a postscript; read verses 28 and 29. From this we may learn how disciples may avoid the tragedy of failure, the tragedy of disappointing the needy and dishonouring God. First, *there must be effective contact with others.* On this point some Christians are like the three on the mountain – occupied with the things of God, but completely unconcerned about reaching others. Other Christians are like the nine – very much in touch with the world, good mixers, living at the ordinary level, but quite unprepared to be tackled with

the genuine spiritual enquiry of a soul in need. Second, *there must be persistent coming to God in prayer*. Only by power received from above can the needy truly be helped. There must be a simple committal to God and a sustained confidence in God expressed in concentrated and continuous praying.

(vii) *The Conclusion*. If then we are to be true disciples of Christ in the work, if we are to stand up to the demands which such discipleship may unexpectedly make on us, we need more readiness to give ourselves to others, to feel concern about their needs, to recognize that there may be someone near at hand who is looking to us for help. We need, also, more determination to give ourselves to prayer in order that we may then help the needy not just in the ordinary social human way but rather in the distinctive Christian spiritual way. For this kind of ministry to the needy can be rendered only by praying.

e. The seeker found (Luke 19:1–10)

NOTE: This passage illustrates how important it is in the proper exposition of Scripture to recognize and set forth the inspired emphasis rather than the natural preference; and to appreciate as complementary the completely opposite sides of the full truth of God's dealings with us and our response to God.

In interpreting this story it is natural with many to give prominence to Zacchaeus, to his initiative in seeking to see Jesus, to his momentous personal decision in freely choosing to receive Jesus into his home. But the inspired record ascribes the initiative to the Saviour. Zacchaeus had his opportunity to see Jesus only because the Saviour chose to pass through Jericho. Zacchaeus had his opportunity to receive Jesus only because the Saviour came to the place where he was, and singled him out by direct personal summons. Not only so; the sequence of events and their issue were under Christ's direct and deliberate control. He virtually took Zacchaeus by storm. There was no saying 'No'. 'I must stay at your house today.' And although the natural opinion of the onlooking crowd was that Jesus had gone to be Zacchaeus' '*guest*', Zacchaeus showed at once that Jesus had come in to be – as he addressed Him – the *Lord* of his life.

So the dominant theme here and the obvious leading thought for a full and balanced exposition is not that Zacchaeus 'wanted to see who Jesus was' (verse 3), but rather, 'For the Son of Man came to seek and to save what was lost' (verse 10). The minor truth is the individual's freedom to choose to embrace God-given opportunities. The major truth is the divine Lord's declared purpose and saving intervention to achieve without hindrance His own predetermined end.

The human mind finds divine sovereignty and pre-destination on the one hand, and human responsibility and freedom to choose on the other hand, difficult to reconcile. The faithful expositor of Scripture needs to be ready to see and to show from this passage and many another that each has its place in the whole truth, and that what God has joined together, ought not to be put asunder.

EXPOSITION: The advent of Christ, the incarnation and appearance in history of the eternal Son of God, is the crowning proof that in all our relations with God the initiative and the decisive action lie with Him, not with us. The opportunities first to seek Him, and then to receive Him, are alike not devised by humans, but God-given, and totally unexpected and undeserved – in other words, all of sovereign grace. This is nowhere more strikingly illustrated than in the record of Zacchaeus and his surprising discovery.

(i) *Christ's personal advent.* 'Jesus entered Jericho and was passing through.' Just as Jerusalem was the city of God and of peace, so to any Jew who knew the Old Testament, Jericho was the city under a curse, a place that had in the past been particularly doomed to destruction. See Joshua 6:21,26. And of all the people in Jericho Zacchaeus had least to commend him; his fellow-citizens described him as 'a sinner'. Yet it was to this town, and for this man, that Jesus came. This incident reflects and expresses the essential wonder of the gospel story; namely, that God Himself came in person to a world under judgment for the benefit of sinners like me, 'to seek and to save what was lost'.

(ii) *The responsive quest.* The advent of Jesus stirred Zacchaeus to action which, as far as he was aware, was entirely independent and wholly due to his own initiative. He heard the news – that Jesus was passing through Jericho – and he determined to see Him for himself. Zacchaeus was the local Commissioner of Taxes and very prosperous, a man very successful in his own estimation. But in this quest he was confronted by a double handicap in relation to others who were equally keen to see Jesus. He was short of stature and he was unpopular. He was not one for whom the crowds would make way. But in his own characteristic way he showed himself to be a man of resourceful independence. He asked noone for help. He did his own seeking. He found his own way of seeing. He gained a position of real advantage from which he was likely to see more than most. Here in a sycamore tree, on the very route he knew Jesus was taking, he waited to achieve his ambition and to see Him.

(iii) *The surprising discovery*. What happened must have been to Zacchaeus a complete surprise, at which he never ceased to wonder. For he had come to see Jesus; actually he was seen by Jesus. He had come on a quest; he found himself the object of Someone else's quest. Jesus treated him as the very man He was looking for. Zacchaeus thought of himself as one of a crowd; he found himself confronted by One who singled him out by name and as if he were the only one there. He came to be a spectator of what Christ was doing; he was called to become a doer under the scrutiny both of Christ and of men and women. The crowd thought that Zacchaeus was the last man to have anything to do with; he was a social outcast, and he knew it. But Jesus chose him out from all the rest and said, 'I must stay at *your* house today.' He had come to where Jesus was passing by intending then to go home alone; he was confronted by One who insisted on coming where he lived and coming to stay. Ordinarily Zacchaeus, like others, would choose and invite his own guests; but this Jesus invited Himself. For other guests Zacchaeus would have time to get ready; but this Jesus took him all unawares, and simply said, imperiously and without warning, 'Now, today, I must come in.'

(iv) *The necessary change*. It was true enough that if Zacchaeus was to welcome Jesus things both in his home and in his life would have to be different. But he was not asked to make them so before Christ came in. He was simply asked to receive Jesus. Change in his life spontaneously burst forth as a result of Christ's presence. 'When you let the Saviour enter, out the sin must go.' Selfishness, greed, dishonest dealing could not live in His presence. Zacchaeus found himself possessed by the desire to act differently. The Lord who had sought him saved him. He had been 'lost'; now he became a true 'son of Abraham' through receiving Jesus. Compare Galatians 3:26,29. So Christ said, 'Today salvation has come to this house.' Christ also said in effect, Let this man be an object lesson. Here is practical evidence of the whole purpose of My mission. 'For the Son of Man came to seek and to save what was lost.'

(v) *The abiding significance*. Let us sum up some of the lessons to be learnt . . .

1. The hope of our salvation lies not in the fact that we are seeking Him, for that by itself would not get us very far; it lies in the fact that He came seeking us. We cannot go where He is; He comes where we are. We have not chosen Him, but He has chosen us.

2. Salvation – becoming a Christian, or fit to be one – is not something we do in order to make ourselves ready for His coming. It is something He does, and does by coming in to make us different.

3. If in His presence we have, like Zacchaeus, a sense of sin and shame and unworthiness, and a new desire to live differently, this is practical proof that 'salvation' has begun.

4. Reception of Christ and response to Him is something to be expressed in our homes and in our daily lives; it is not something we do only in a detached kind of way when we go for an hour to church on Sundays.

5. Jesus Himself is salvation. It is His presence that makes us different. It is when and where He is received that it is true to say, Now ('this day') and here ('this house') salvation is come.

6

Expounding Short Statements

Single verses or short statements of the Bible provide a second type of material for exposition; and their treatment, once seriously undertaken, can provide the would-be expositor with both rigorous initial discipline and rewarding ultimate achievement. For, on the one hand, if one is to be true to the task of exposition, one must stay in study and thought within the confines of the text, and not wander off at a tangent to other ideas. But, on the other hand, particularly when one chooses one of the very many short texts, which readily break apart, and lend themselves to analytical exposition, one begins to discover by practice and experience how fruitful and satisfying such exclusive pursuit of true exposition can become.

Our concern, therefore, in this chapter is to illustrate how such short texts can be expounded, and to indicate the way in which exposition of this kind will determine the whole structure and content of a sermon.

The adoption of this method of treatment means that, instead of using a quotation from the Bible as a peg on which to hang a string of ideas collected from elsewhere, the chosen text itself is allowed to provide the ideas. In this way the preacher becomes a true minister or servant of the Word. He makes it his business to take the text to pieces to analyse its content, to examine it from every angle, to seek to appreciate the full significance of its distinctive phraseology, and thus, so to speak, to put it under pressure and make it yield up all its treasure. Sometimes when in this way it is examined closely as under a microscope, the text will offer new suggestions, not originally in the preacher's own mind, or will indicate that, in order properly to complete the treatment of the subject under consideration, other ideas should be included. The preacher will then follow these new lines of thought instead of concentrating on independent preferences of his own.

This method ought most of all to appeal to all who believe – what the Bible itself teaches – that it is the Scripture, or written Word, which is 'God-breathed' (see 2 Tim. 3:16) and is the direct product of the creative activity of the divine Spirit. It is such conviction, that the written Word matters, that the expression of truth in words which we find in the Bible is divinely significant, that can become the driving force to constrain first the preacher, and then his hearers, to the necessary intellectual effort fully to pursue expository understanding and appreciation. For often the reason why this kind of exposition is neither attempted in the pulpit, nor welcomed in the pews, is just laziness, or lack of sufficient sustained interest. It seems easier, and on the surface more attractive, to use other methods. But this method yields richer rewards.

Let's now seek to show by actual illustration how readily some scriptural statements break apart, and how their pieces provide obvious subsections for an instructive analytical exposition.

Example 1: Romans 1:16
In this verse Paul confesses his personal conviction about the gospel. He tells us why he is not ashamed of it. 'Because it is' he says, 'the power of God for the salvation of everyone who believes.' Notice here that these last words tell us five truths about the gospel.

(i) *Its character.* It is 'the power' or 'dynamic' (Gk. *dunamis*); i.e. it is not philosophy, a list of rules, or mere good advice and exhortation, but transforming energy.

(ii) *Its origin.* It is 'of God'; i.e. it is not devised by us, not another human attempt to achieve the humanly impossible, but wrought by God.

(iii) *Its benefit.* It is 'for the salvation'. It offers both rescue from an evil state, and restoration to full health and well-being.

(iv) *Its universality; and its individual appeal.* It is 'of everyone', the Jew and the Greek. It is not restricted to one race, class, or type. It affords an opportunity which all can and must embrace for their own sakes.

(v) *Its one condition of benefit*, and therefore *its simplicity* and *its suitability*. It is to them 'who believes'. It does not demand of us works, merit, money, brains, culture, etc., which are beyond our producing, but simply asks for the response of faith.

Example 2: 1 Peter 2:21
In his first epistle Peter shows that the sufferings of Christ, which had at first been completely unwelcome to him, had become central to his whole thought and understanding of the Christian gospel. The three main

ideas which he had learnt, and which are treated in various ways in 1 Peter, are all summed up together in eight words in 1 Peter 2:21: 'Christ suffered for you, leaving you an example.'

(i) *'Christ suffered.'* His suffering was not an unfortunate tragedy and an awful mistake, but the proper fulfilment of His fore-ordained course as God's *Christ*.

(ii) *'For you.'* The reason why He, the sinless, bore the extreme penalty of sin, right up to public execution 'on the tree', was that He 'bare *our* sins' not His own. He did it 'for you'.

(iii) *'Leaving you an example.'* The pathway Christ trod in this world provides for all who would follow Him a pattern to be copied. Disciples must also take up their cross.

Example 3: Hebrews 11:7
For ease of reference here is the verse in full: 'By faith Noah, when warned about things not yet seen, in holy fear built an ark to save his family. By his faith he condemned the world and became heir of the righteousness that comes by faith.' Note the following four main points:

(i) *What stirred faith to express itself.* 'When warned about things not yet seen' i.e. there was a special divine revelation, the God-given word.

(ii) *Why faith was necessary.* The warning was 'of things not yet seen'. The revelation concerned the unseen and the future. Compare Hebrews 11:1.

(iii) How faith expressed itself. Note that Noah's faith was no mere theoretical assent, but a responsive activity.

First he was 'in holy fear'; 'he reverently gave heed' (Weymouth). Second, he 'built an ark', i.e. he got ready. His action corresponded to what the revelation said was impending.

(iv) *Results of faith's activity.* Note, first, the physical deliverance of his family. His action led to the saving of his family. In the second place it resulted in his own justification in the sight of God. He 'became heir of the righteousness that comes by faith'. Thirdly, by his witness he left others without excuse. He 'condemned the world'.

In order to provide more detailed illustration of methods of treatment we now offer an extended exposition of several short statements. The preliminary explanatory notes indicate in each particular case significant features which are in principle of general application to the treatment of other similar statements.

a. The way of relief for the burdened (Psalm 55:2)

NOTE: In this treatment general features are first identified, features common to many biblical statements. They are, first, the recognition of the need of humans – life has burdens; second, there is a declaration of the grace of God – He shall sustain thee. Then, by moving closer to this particular statement, its more distinctive truths or emphases are identified. We note, first, that burdens bring us to God; second, that burdens allow us to prove God's mercy and power in giving us aid; third, that there are here both an imperative command and a promise of divine aid addressed to the individual – 'Cast *your* cares . . . and he will sustain *you.*' Finally, by moving closer still, one finds in the actual phraseology of this particular statement aspects of truth which can be discerned in a special way from this one verse, possibly perhaps as from no other. It is such discovery and corresponding treatment of the detail peculiar to each particular text, which gives to such full and painstaking exposition attractive freshness of content. In this way a very familiar general truth may be preached with an arresting and suggestive new emphasis, or with a different and an illuminating fresh slant both in interpretation and application.

EXPOSITION: 'Cast thy burden upon the Lord, and he shall sustain thee.' (KJV) Here is a word for a burdened soul. It is because it contains advice such as this that the Bible is of such practical value. It faces the facts of life. It abounds in stories of people in trouble. *Life has burdens*; God's Word does not deny it.

What, then, can be the reason for such burdens? Why does a loving, heavenly Father allow them to press upon us? The first answer is that they are sent in order to bring us down by something too much for us, so that we are constrained to come to God. When the sun is shining, and everything is prosperous, we tend to forget God. We imagine we can get on without Him. He often drops out of our lives and thoughts. But when distress and disaster shake us out of fancied security and false confidences down to a desperate sense of need, instinctively we cry to God. This is one great value of trouble. This is why distress is such a frequent method of divine discipline. It keeps us close to God. It brings us back to Him. *Burdens are meant to be cast upon Him*.

Why does God allow burdens to press upon us? There is a further answer. Trouble not only brings us to God; it gives God an opportunity to display His power. It is when we in our despair bring our burdens to God that we find He can carry them all. None are too heavy for

Him. So when burdens press, do not look despairingly at it. Look instead for the help. Cast thy burden upon the Lord, and *He shall sustain thee*.

Cast thy burden upon the Lord. This is no mere gentle advice. It is not just a kindly suggestion. It is an abrupt, urgent imperative. It demands active obedience. More than that, the word 'cast' is a violent word, indicating the use of effort. It means 'to fling' or 'to hurl'. It commands us to exert all our energies, to stir ourselves to forceful effort, and to hurl our load of care upon God. Why such language? Why this call to energetic effort and decisive action?

There are two reasons for such an urgent imperative. The first is that anxiety and despair take some shifting. We are so prone to let them settle down in our hearts as permanent residents. We are so unwilling to believe that it is possible to get rid of them. So, unless we act powerfully, unless we stir ourselves to the effort of getting rid of them, we shall go on carrying them. There is an old story of a traveller with a burden who was given a lift by a passing cart. When asked why he did not remove his load, and put it down on the cart, he said: 'It was so very kind of you to give me a lift. I did not know you would carry my bundle too.' We say, 'How stupid!' Yet how often some of us behave in just this way. We are trusting Christ for our soul's salvation, but still carrying ourselves all our own daily anxieties. For such people nothing less than a violent effort will suffice to give them freedom. They need awakening to energetic action. So for them – for any of us who are still carrying our load of care – this imperative word is written. *Cast* thy burden. Get rid of it. With a decisive effort of will and faith pitch it off your back. Carry it no longer. Here and now, once and for all, holding nothing back, cast it upon Jesus; and be free.

There is a second reason why such a pressing command is necessary. For, if we do not get rid of our burden, it will do more than weigh us down. It will harden our hearts. It will become our grievance. In the Hebrew the word translated 'burden' means 'that which is given'. For the thought about trouble which perplexes us and causes us offence is just this, that God allows it. Yes, says this verse, that is so. He has given it to you. Immediately we ask, Why? and next we murmur and complain, and drift away from God, because we feel He has dealt harshly and unjustly with us. The urgent imperative of Psalm 55:22 is aimed at preventing such a development. It calls us to act at once, to get rid of our burden before it hardens our hearts. For if God gave it to you – then it is His. He is only testing you to see what you will do with it. Imagine a father giving his small girl some things to carry. He gives her one too heavy, which the girl cannot possibly manage. What does the girl do? She gives it back and says, 'You must carry this one, Daddy.'

So, when our heavenly Father gives us a burden, something more than we can carry, something that begins at once to weigh us down, something that threatens to break not only our back but our submissive spirit, what are we to do? Act at once. Rise up, and throw it back upon Him. Cast thy burden upon the Lord. Then, not only will He carry *the burden*. He will do more. He shall sustain *you*.

b. 'You are to give him the name Jesus' (Matthew 1:21)

NOTE: The treatment of this verse illustrates the value of, and indeed the necessity of reference to, and comparison with, other passages for the full understanding of all that one particular statement may imply in its biblical context. Such reference and comparison are in such cases a desirable part of full exposition. The Bible should therefore be treated often as its own best dictionary or commentary; and understanding should be increased by comparing verse with verse.

EXPOSITION: 'She will give birth to a son, and you are to give him the name JESUS, because he will save his people from their sins.' When people hear that a baby has been born, one of the first questions they ask is, 'What is the baby to be called?' This is a matter of unfailing interest. It is one of the inevitable demands that having children of our own makes upon us – to give the child a name. Among us it is common to look back or look around and to call the child after somebody. It is more Eastern and particularly more biblical to look forward, and to call the child by a name which will have some significance and fulfilment in his life, as our Lord re-named Simon, and called him Peter. Further, to the God-fearing and the spiritually minded, it was sometimes the practice to look up, and by a name given or adopted to express faith in God, and sometimes to register a new and special relation to God. So, after Jacob's encounter with the angel of God, his own name was changed to 'Israel', and he called the name of the place 'Peniel'. (See Genesis 32:24–30.) Or again, at a time of great national peril in Judah in the days of Ahaz, a mother called her child 'Emmanuel'. In this way she expressed her faith that there was hope for the future both for the child and for the nation because '*God is with us*'. This, said the prophet Isaiah, for those who have the faith to embrace it, is a sign from God, a sure promise that God will save His people. (See Isaiah 7:1–16.)

This last sign was, as we know, in the purposes of God to have a more distant and far greater fulfilment in the birth of the long-expected Messiah. Let's then consider what we are to learn from the name given to the Child of Bethlehem. If we are, so to speak, to name Him afresh for ourselves, let us consider by what name Christians call Him, and why. Let us then seek to discover from the Scriptures some significant truths concerning His name 'Jesus'.

(i) *His name was made known by revelation.* Joseph and Mary did not choose it. They were guided by God to the right name. This indicates a truth which applies to us all. Left to our natural judgment, none of us would give this baby the right name. When He was born the only people who appreciated who He really was were those divinely enlightened. Similarly, if I want to see and know the real truth about the Child of Bethlehem, I must ask God to open my eyes.

(ii) *His name was to be understood from Scripture.* To those who knew the Jewish Scriptures the name 'Jesus', in its Hebrew form 'Joshua', was a familiar one. It was a name of outstanding significance specially given to its first holder (see Numbers 13:16). By adding a divine prefix to his original name, Moses suggested that Joshua was that man whom Jehovah would use to save His people. Certainly it is true that this name 'Joshua' stands out in the Old Testament as the name of leaders of God's people at the times of the two great entries of God's people into the promised land, first in the original conquest of Canaan, and centuries later in the return of the exiles from Babylon. (See Deuteronomy 31:23; Ezra 3:1,2.) The fresh naming of a child by this name suggested, therefore, that the time and the man for a new activity of divine redemption for God's people had arrived.

(iii) *His name explained both as indicating His work, and as disclosing His Person.* The angel said to Joseph, 'You are to give him the name JESUS, because he will save his people from their sins.' His work was to save the people of God. Israel's day of redemption was at hand. This salvation was to bring not material prosperity and earthly empire, but moral purity and peace with God. It was to be a salvation not of the earthly Jerusalem from the Roman oppressor, but of the souls of men and women from the bondage of sin.

Again, the angel did not say that His name meant that Jehovah would use Jesus to save Jehovah's people; but that this Jesus would save *His own* people. There is no distinction of two persons; the human agent and the divine Author of salvation, the human deliverer and the divine Lord of the people, are One and the Same. To those who have eyes to see, therefore, these words mean that this Jesus is God Himself come in person to save His own people. He is the true Emmanuel – God with us. So, says the evangelist, the sign, given in the days of Isaiah, with a limited earthly reference as a token of faith in God and His deliverance of His people, finds in this child its perfect and final fulfilment as the right name for God incarnate, the personal divine Deliverer. This 'Jesus' is our 'Emmanuel'. (See Matthew 1:22,23.)

(iv) *His name believed in by His people.* Our personal attitude to this name as His name is one of the practical tests of our membership in the company of His saved people. For those who find deliverance and life are those who 'believe on his name' (John 1:12). His name 'Jesus' sums up for us as nothing else can, both who He is and what He has done and, therefore, what He is to us. This name tells me that He is God, the Saviour. Rightly to call Him 'my Jesus' is to acknowledge Him as 'my God and my

Saviour'. This is something each believing soul must do for himself or herself – to call His name Jesus. Have you celebrated not only His birth, but also His death and resurrection and exaltation to the throne by calling Him this – your 'Jesus'?

Finally, is it any wonder that Charles Wesley longed for a thousand tongues to sing:

> Jesus! the name that charms our fears,
> That bids our sorrows cease;
> 'Tis music in the sinner's ears,
> 'Tis life, and health, and peace.

Or do you wonder either that he went on to pray:

> My gracious Master and my God,
> Assist me to proclaim,
> To spread through all the earth abroad
> The honours of Thy name.

c. Christ's twofold offer of rest (Matthew 11:28–30)

NOTE: In this passage there are two features which demand careful exposition if they are to be rightly understood and fully appreciated.

(i) *Apparent repetition*. At first sight the same promise of rest seems simply to be twice repeated by the Saviour. But attention to the detail of the phraseology discloses that there is a distinct and important difference between the two promises. The two experiences of rest are not identical but complementary. Similarly elsewhere in the Scriptures apparent repetitions commonly make significant addition by double statement and do not just merely repeat the same single idea. It is the task and the privilege of the expositor first himself to win entrance, and then to lead others, into this enriching larger understanding.

(ii) *Apparent contradiction*. These words of our Lord confront us with paradoxical juxtaposition of two normally contradictory and mutually exclusive claims. On the one hand, Christ makes a sweeping pretentious claim Himself to be able to give rest to any and to all who are burdened. On the other hand, He professes in spirit to be submissive and dependent, neither self-assertive nor self-confident. When the Scriptures thus confront us with apparent contradiction, what needs to be recognized is that both statements are true; and that the fullness of revealed truth is to be appreciated, and its blessings enjoyed, only as the truth of both is realized and responded to.

EXPOSITION: 'Come unto me, all ye that labour and are heavy laden, and I will give you rest. Take my yoke upon you, and learn of me; for I am meek and lowly in heart: and ye shall find rest unto your souls. For my yoke is easy, and my burden is light.' (KJV) These wonderful, familiar words of our Lord are words which by repeated mention offer us one supreme reward – the reward of *rest*. Let us notice at once not only that the word 'rest' comes twice, but also that two kinds of rest are here offered to us, one *rest from labour* and the other *rest in labour*. Christ's first word tells the overburdened and the diseased how to get relief and restoration of health. His second word tells the restored and the healthy how to live so as to keep free from disease and distress of spirit. In other words, the great Physician here makes a twofold offer – first to make us well, and then to show us how to keep well not merely in body but in soul.

(i) *The Offerer of rest.* Here it is the Lord Jesus who speaks; and He puts all the emphasis upon *Himself.* 'Come unto *me*', He says; 'and I will give you rest. Take *my* yoke . . . and learn of *me*. . . . For *my* yoke is easy.' Here we have evidence both of the unique simplicity and of the distinctive exclusiveness of true New Testament Christianity. This rest is to be found in Christ and in Him alone. His own words, which precede this offer of rest, make plain how it is that He can make such stupendous claims: first, because He is the eternal Son of God; second, because He is the appointed Mediator between God and men; third, because He can bring people into the personal knowledge of God (see verse 27).

(ii) *The offer of rest from labour.* This is fundamentally an offer to deal with the state of things which is causing us weariness and strain, and to bring it decisively to an end. For He can deliver us from ceaseless, unsatisfying work, from the works of self-righteousness. In some cases this may also be interpreted as an offer to give those, who are worn out and overburdened with too much doing, the kind of temporary rest or relief, which will bring necessary refreshment of spirit and renewal of strength to work again.

This kind of benefit is a gift, something done for us by Christ alone. It is not something we can produce. It needs His hand and His action. He does not say, 'Do this' or 'Try that', but '*I will*'; just as a surgeon might say, 'You must let me operate, if you want relief.' All I have to do is to come to Him, and to put myself in His hands. Also, this kind of benefit can be enjoyed only if I am willing for the wrong thing to be removed by His hands, like a troublesome tooth which I must let the dentist take out; or only if I am willing for my 'busy-ness' to be interrupted by the kind of rest which will really renew. For

the stressed soul in a state of spiritual weariness Christ
is the one and only sufficient and satisfying resting-
place. I must do what Mary did, and what Martha
would not do – drop my work to sit at His feet. So the
prophet wrote, 'Even youths grow tired and weary . . .
but those who hope in the LORD will renew their
strength' (Is. 40:30,31).

(iii) *The offer of rest in labour*. Here Christ invites us to
change our yoke, to give up one form of service and to
enter another, to have done with the burdensome toil of
self-effort and to submit to direct, personal control from
above, like an animal under the yoke; and to find in this
new way of living a form of service that is not exhaust-
ing and burdensome, but restful and rewarding, satisfying to the soul, a veritable delight. To this end, Christ
says, a new spirit or attitude is needed. And this attitude
He not only inculcates in His teaching, but also exemplifies in His own earthly life. So He says, 'Learn of me; for
I am meek and lowly in heart.' What matters is right
heart-attitude towards God; learning to live as a submissive and dependent creature, delighting in God's
direction and counting on God's power. So shall I find
rest for my soul. For the way of realized peace in the
midst of the work of His service is to follow God's guidance in submission, and to accept God's grace in
dependence.

(iv) *The way therefore to enjoy rest*. To enjoy rest from
labour and renewal of strength for life's tasks I need to
come to Christ, to trust in Him. To enjoy rest in labour,
and quietness of spirit to go on doing God's will, I need
a spirit of submissive dependence and responsive obedience. In other words, the twofold secret of enjoying
Christ's twofold rest is *to trust and to obey Him*. (Scripture

repeatedly confronts us with warnings that it is possible to know what to do to enjoy God's rest, and yet to refuse to trust and to obey, and so to fail to enter in. Read Is. 30:15; Jer. 6:16; Heb. 3:18 – 4:2 and 4:9–11.)

d. Entering into the significance of the Lord's Supper
(1 Corinthians 11:26)

NOTE: If our Christian understanding and use of the Lord's Supper are to be truly scriptural, the statements of Scripture about it are an important subject for full and faithful exposition. On the one hand, explicit New Testament references to the subject are relatively few. On the other hand, the attempt is often made to justify wrong faith and practice with regard to it by an appeal to the wording of Scripture. For instance, our Lord's words 'This is my body' are said to support the doctrine of transubstantiation. Do this 'in remembrance of me' is said to mean 'Offer this before God as a memorial of my sacrifice'.

The only effective answer to such misinterpretation and misrepresentation is careful, positive exposition in detail of exactly what is written in the New Testament. We ought to be able to show, not from inherited church tradition, and still less from our own ideas or preferences, but rather from the written Word of God what God intended His people to believe and to do. We ought, also, to be willing to bring the practice of our own congregation under the judgment of the Word of God, and to let it be tested by this standard. This surely is the way in which to establish individual believers in the ability to discern for themselves whether current church faith and practice are truly scriptural. Expository preaching and teaching of this sort is the healthy way to promote, where it is needed, desirable and possibly long overdue reformation.

EXPOSITION: 'For as often as you eat this bread, and drink the cup, you proclaim the Lord's death until he comes' (RSV).

(i) 'The Lord's death.' Participation in the Lord's Supper unquestionably calls us to remember, and to focus our attention upon, what is here called, in a striking phrase, 'the Lord's death'. We may well pause to contemplate its paradoxical character, its staggering wonder – that the Lord, He who is eternal God, He who is now the exalted King of the universe, enthroned on high, not only lived as a true man here on earth, but also in a body of flesh and blood like ours actually experienced a shameful death, and was publicly executed, as if He were a criminal, by crucifixion. Not only so, we are meant in our use of this service still more wonderfully to recognize and to confess that this death of the Lord has for us value which is personal, decisive, abiding, and eternal. Let's then consider what this verse indicates that we ought knowingly and deliberately to do, if we are to participate correctly.

(ii) 'This bread.' We are, first, commanded by the Lord to do something with 'this bread', that is, the bread which He Himself broke, and of which He said, not simply 'This is my *body*, but 'This is my body *broken*' or 'given'; and 'broken *for you*'. Those who participate with this in mind cannot but recognize that the Lord knowingly went to this shameful end on our behalf, in our place, and for our benefit. As in the feeding of the five thousand, the *breaking* of the loaves was the point at which the miracle happened and the bread was made more than enough for all; so the breaking of our Lord's body in death is the point from and through which He is able to meet all the needs of all. So by eating 'this bread' we ought to confess that we believe that Christ can and does and will save us because He died for us.

(iii) *'The cup.'* We are, secondly, to do something with 'the cup' of which Christ said, 'This cup is the new covenant in my blood' (11:25, RSV). According to ancient Semitic ritual, covenants were sealed by death, by dividing the pieces of slain animals and passing between them. (See Genesis 15:8–21; Jeremiah 34:18,19.) So here Christ spoke symbolically of His death by dividing the pieces, and keeping the bread and wine separate; and then He asserted that this death of His would ratify the new covenant of God, and would make its benefits available to be enjoyed by God's people. Put simply, these benefits are cleansing and quickening – remission of sins and the power of the indwelling Spirit to enable us to do God's will. So those who drink this cup of the new covenant ought to do so in expression of their faith that Christ's death ratified this covenant and that its promises can in consequence be fulfilled in their experience.

(iv) 'Until he comes.' Thirdly, what we therefore do in this service we are only to do 'until he comes'. In other words, this activity is transitory, not final. It ministers to the present need; it is not the ultimate goal. For, when the Lord gave His disciples these very symbols of the broken bread and the cup, He anticipated the ultimate issue of His sacrifice, and spoke of the coming triumph feast in His Father's kingdom. So we ought in this service consciously to confess that we believe that Christ's death is not only the ground of the beginning of salvation, and the guarantee of its daily continuance, but also that it holds sure promise of a crowning consummation. We should, therefore, anticipate the glory that shall be

revealed, in which, because of Christ's death for us, we
are to share.

(v) 'As often as you eat . . . and drink.' We will now
notice carefully what is the action in which we are to
share, which is capable of such deep and far-reaching
significance. We are to eat and to drink, to partake of the
bread and wine. This is the simple and single and sufficient use of this service. There is here no mention of a
movement towards God. There is no sacrifice of the
altar; it is a meal or feast from the Lord's table. Also, it is
insufficient just to behold in contemplative reverence.
There is no place for non-communicating attendance.
The service demands participation in the bread and
wine. The appointed way to proclaim the Lord's death
till He comes is to eat and to drink. Further, such participation is meant to express outwardly our appropriation
by faith of all that Christ's death makes ours in relation
to the past, the present and the future – in relation to sin,
present life in this world, and our hope of glory.

(vi) 'You proclaim the Lord's death.' Finally, when we
eat and drink in this way, we are intended to 'proclaim
the Lord's death'. This implies that the main action of
this service is not something which the minister alone
does with the elements at the Table; it is something
which we all do, or should do, when we eat and drink.
Also, the word 'proclaim' is a strong and dramatic one.
It at least suggests that we are to act a meaning; that we
are openly to exhibit our attitude to, and our confidence
in, Christ's death by what we do with 'this bread' and
'the cup'. One wonders whether it may be possible to go
even further. The Greek word translated 'proclaim' is
often used of spoken utterance. Does it suggest that,
when they partook, the Corinthian Christians made a

declaration concerning the significance of their action? Just as, when at a wedding, say of a couple named John and Sarah, their health is proposed, we show our concurrence and desire for their well-being not only by drinking, but also by declaring 'John and Sarah!' so one wonders whether Paul means that, as they ate and drank in the Lord's Supper, they made some declaration of faith concerning the Lord's death. Certainly in the administration of the Holy Communion, according to the Church of England Prayer Book order, I have sometimes wished that the communicant could (with appropriate slight alteration) use the second half of the words of administration to express his or her responsive and appropriating faith. This would mean that, after the minister delivering the bread had said, 'The Body of our Lord Jesus Christ, which was given for thee, preserve thy body and soul unto everlasting life', the individual receiving would respond, 'I take and eat this in remembrance that Christ died for me, and I feed on Him in my heart by faith with thanksgiving'. But, whether such open declaration be intended in 1 Corinthians 11:26 or not, it is surely this kind of faith and heart response in the recipient which are indispensable, if, as he eats and drinks, he is worthily to 'proclaim the Lord's death'.

e. Marriage: its place and its pattern (Genesis 2:24 and Ephesians 5:31)

NOTE: Here we have a very important statement which occurs in three different places in the Scriptures. Not only does it occur in both the Old Testament and in the New; but also in the latter it is quoted twice, first by Jesus (as Matthew 19:5 and Mark 10:7 both record), and later by the apostle Paul. And while the Old Testament and Jesus both refer in its use to God's purpose in creation, the apostle in his use of it is comparing the union of husband and wife to God's pattern in redemption for Christ and the church.

There are, therefore, illustrated here two typical characteristics of the Bible to which proper exposition must give appropriate attention; first, the way in which what is written in the Old Testament finds its final endorsement and full divine confirmation in Christ and the New Testament; and second, the way in which God's earthly purpose and the manifestation of His wisdom and grace in the present natural creation is complemented and consummated by His heavenly purpose, and by His crowning work of redemption and resurrection in Christ and in the new spiritual creation.

It is one of the keynotes of discerning Christian biblical exposition to be alert to discern, and ready to set forth, the frequent occurrences of such significant characteristics as these – namely, the anticipation of the New Testament in the Old, the fulfilment and authentication of the Old Testament in the New, the complementary glories of God's work in creation and redemption, the illustrations in nature of parallel methods of God's work in grace, and above all, the finding in Christ by the Spirit of the true expression and fulfilment of every transitory earthly figure of heavenly and eternal truth.

EXPOSITION: 'For this reason a man will leave his father and mother and be united to his wife, and the two will become one flesh' (Eph. 5:31). These words refer, of course, to the action of a man in getting married. They indicate why it should be done. If, therefore, we look at the context of these words, we may expect to find out something about the ground and the purpose of marriage. The words occur first in Genesis 2:24, and were quoted from that passage by our Lord as words of God, the Creator (see Matthew 19:4, 5). In Ephesians 5:31 they occur again. In seeking to understand this repetition we may rightly distinguish a twofold reference – first, to the divinely-ordained place of marriage, and second, to its God-given pattern.

(i) *The place of marriage.* The first reference of this statement concerns the fundamental justification of marriage; it indicates the reason for giving it the place that it holds in human relations. *This is found in the divine ordering of creation*, and in God's plan and purpose as the Creator. For when God made man He made us male and female. He took the woman out of the man to provide a helpmate for the man, and a help of such an intimate character as to be his 'other half'. Therefore, it is right, it is what God the Creator intended, that a man should find human completion and fulfilment by leaving his parents to get married. This fundamental truth about human life is something whose significance we all need to recognize – especially those who get married and their parents. Let us consider two of its aspects.

First, marriage is *a divine ordinance*. The witness of Scripture makes plain that getting married is not just our idea. It is not merely an expression of the initiative and free choice of the couple concerned. Rather, getting married is only doing what God the Creator has foreordained should be done. For He made us male and female. Our capacity and our desire for marriage are God-given. Therefore, the only wise and right way to live the married life is to seek to learn from God's Word, by submission to His guidance, how it should be done. So, in a Christian wedding, the first thing the man and the woman do together as husband and wife is to kneel in prayer – a practice which they will often repeat. Also, since it is God the Creator who has thus joined man and woman together in marriage, we have no right to order, and still less to break apart, the marriage relation just to please themselves. So our Lord explicitly declared, 'Therefore what God has joined together, let man not separate.'

Secondly, the marriage relation is *the primary social loyalty*. It is by coming together in marriage that a man and woman become parents, and a new family is established. Therefore, the crowning fulfilment of marriage is to see one's children entering into the same completion, and leaving one home to start another. So parents should regard the marriage of their children not as loss but as gain. Also, until a man or woman gets married, their first human duty is to their parents. But, once he or she does get married, from then on the married partner comes first. So, as the Word of God plainly states, a man has and ought, in some sense, to forsake his nearest – to leave his father and mother – in order to join to his wife. The one person a married person should never relinquish is his wife – or her husband. Family life can only become stable and remain secure when, in devotion to and care for one another, husband and wife through thick and thin in this way stick together – 'till death do them part'.

(ii) *The pattern for marriage*. The second reference of our text concerns the practice of married life, the pattern of its fulfilment, the way to enter into it worthily and richly. By the Christian, by the saved sinner who by God's grace and Christ's death has become a member of Christ's church, *this pattern is found in the divine ordering of redemption*, in God's work as the Redeemer. For here at a higher level, and in a mystical or spiritually allegorical sense, the incarnate Son of God has taken the company of the redeemed to be, as it were, a part of Himself – to be His bride, and to belong to His body, to be 'of His flesh and of His bones'. It is, therefore, in the fulfilment of this relation between Christ and His church that the Christian husband and wife are taught to find the supreme pattern for living together and living for one another. (Try reading thoughtfully Ephesians 5:22–25.)

The pattern for the husband is *loving self-sacrifice*. The pattern for the wife is *reverent submission and devotion*. The husband is to forget himself and to hold nothing back in caring for the wife. The wife is to find satisfaction and fulfilment in giving herself to serve the will and the well-being of her husband. This means that in married life, responsibility to lead or to steer rests with the man; and their full sticking together will only continue if the woman is a devoted follower, delighting in obeying. Yet this does not give to the man any right to be self-centred or self-indulgent. The lead which he sets for the woman he is to set in true self-forgetful love, in concern for God's glory and for her good rather than his own. One may think in illustration of a man and woman riding on a tandem bicycle. Here the man rides in front, and the woman should gladly follow and support his lead. But all the time the man has to remember the woman behind him, and to let what they undertake together be determined by her comfort and by the limits of her strength.

So true marriage is *a divinely-intended school of unselfishness, and a daily challenge to its practice*. Its crowning paradox is that in the hour when each gets a life partner to lean upon, each is called in a new and lifelong way to begin to give. The secret of happy and fruitful married life is found in giving – first, in giving to one another, second, in giving to their children, third, in giving to all whom they welcome into their home. Above all, and through all, it is found in giving to the Lord

Himself *in reverent submission and devotion and in loving self-sacrifice*, remembering the words the Lord Jesus himself said, 'It is more blessed to give than to receive' (Acts 20:35).

7

Expounding Longer Passages

A third type of material for exposition is the longer con-
secutive passage, particularly the kind of reasoned
sequence of thought to be found in the prophetical
books or the epistles, and, in a somewhat different way,
in the Psalms or in comparable poetic sections of the
Bible. Such passages are unquestionably the most difficult to expound effectively until you acquire some proficiency in the art. But that is no reason for allowing
oneself to be frightened off making an attempt. For one
discovers the rewarding worth of such study and ministry chiefly by doing it; and in this, as in such everyday
pursuits as learning to ride a bicycle, to use a typewriter
or to speak a foreign language, it is practice and diligent
application that counts. Such exposition of a whole passage, if it is to grip and hold attention and to compel
responsive interest, if it is to make a definite impression,
and exert an effective influence upon hearers, must be
something more than disjointed comment verse by
verse. What is essential is a synthetic approach. The necessary analysis and explanation of details must be kept
subservient to the coherence of a dominant theme. One
needs to discover the connecting thread of a passage on
which its varying points can harmoniously be strung

together, and in relation to which each detail may find its place and its point.

Such unified and coherent treatment of a passage can be helped for both preacher and hearers by the choice (if it proves possible, as it often does) from the passage of a short pivot sentence (called in the illustrative outlines on pages 59 and 94 a 'short text'), by which to emphasize, and around which to develop, the dominant theme. Its idea should then be expanded and developed within the passage or context, so that it becomes unmistakably obvious to the hearers that they are being given in detail the fullness and the force of the passage as a whole. The preacher's aim should therefore be to weave into the full structure of his exposition all the relevant and usable points of the whole paragraph or chosen section of Scripture.

In detailed illustration of methods of treatment we now offer extended exposition of several longer passages, together with some explanatory comment.

a. A challenge to re-affirm our decision to serve the Lord (Joshua 24:14–25)

NOTE: Here the historical setting and the distinctive character of the passage need to be clearly explained and somewhat forcibly emphasized. It was a very solemn occasion – Joshua's last charge. He pressed upon the Israelites a very searching challenge; a challenge enforced by refusal to be satisfied with simple and possibly superficial assent, and a challenge driven home by repeated demand upon them, both to face the cost and solemnly to pledge their word.

The dialogue character of the passage should be thrown into clear relief; the first demand and the people's answer, the urgent warning against apostasy and the serious answering declaration of single and undivided loyalty, and finally the practical demand upon them to confirm their professed choice by corresponding uncompromising words and actions.

EXPOSITION: The outline which follows provides an example of the formal homiletical treatment to which reference was made on page 118.

b. Answering the expectation of the needy (Mark 9:14–29)

NOTE: In the exposition of this passage illustration is briefly afforded of the seven constituent parts of full homiletical treatment. These seven parts are:

(i) *The Text*. Joshua 24:14–25: especially verses 14 and 15; so that a possible 'short text' would be 'Serve him with all faithfulness'; *or* ''Now fear the LORD and serve him with all faithfulness . . . But if serving the LORD seems undesirable to you, then choose for yourselves this day whom you will serve, . . . But as for me and my household, we will serve the LORD.'

(ii) *The Explanation*. Joshua 24 records Joshua's final charge to representatives of all the people of Israel. His obvious concern before his death was to get them to give to God, and permanently to pledge to Him, true and wholehearted service. So he confronted them with the devotion which God deserves, and with the dedication which His service demands.

(iii) *The Introduction*. This exhortation still has obvious relevance as the present word of God. Much of our religion is also superficial and half-hearted, not sincere and wholehearted. We are not truly committed Christians. Our loyalty to Christ is not complete, undivided and unchanging. We share outwardly in the public worship of God on Sunday. Daily and more privately we acknowledge Him. Yet there are parts of our day or week, even whole areas of our lives, in which other gods have power over us, or we worship idols. The passage we are now to study makes plain what God had to say to the Israelites on this very issue. It is for us to take His word to heart, and to apply it to our own lives.

(iv) *The Proposition.* So let's in our present study seek here both to find and to face *a challenge to re-affirm our decision to serve the Lord.*

(v) *The Divisions.* Joshua fundamentally insisted on two essentials: first, the devotion which God deserves (verse 14), and secondly, the decision to be faced by the people (verse 15). In reply the people acknowledge a debt to be remembered, and assert that, because of it, to do anything other than serve God is unthinkable; so their decision is without question to serve the Lord (verses 16–18).

Joshua nevertheless presses upon them the exacting demands of such service. There is a price to be paid, and a danger to be feared. This calls forth in still more emphatic terms the profession from the people of a decision which is unmistakable (verses 19–21).

Again Joshua is not fully satisfied. He regards the issues involved as so momentous that he urges that their decision and all that it involves should be seriously pledged and confirmed by supporting action. So he speaks of a dedication to be covenanted (verses 22–25). (These statements, not finally reduced to short sub-headings, are intended to show how appreciation of the sequence of ideas in the passage leads to the distinction of its separate parts, and the tentative formation of appropriate descriptive phrases. Before moving on to the final form of presentation to others in *The Development*, one must settle on the most useful sub-headings; and beware of the temptation to be either too clever or too complicated!)

(vi) *The Development.*

1. *The devotion which God deserves*. Read verse 14. God, if He is to be properly acknowledged at all, must be reverenced as God. Our worship should be genuine; not a superficial ceremonial performance only, but the expression of a deep personal heart response. Unless He is our only God, and Lord of all, He is not really our Lord and our God at all. Devotion to Him demands the deliberate renunciation of all other gods. We must have done with idols. In this realm of worship it is impossible to serve God *and* something else. On this very issue our Lord Himself quoted to the tempter the decisive scriptural words: 'Worship the Lord your God, and serve him only' (Matt. 4:10).

2. *The decision to be faced*. Read verse 15. The consequent challenge here is to be all or none, to be clear-cut in one's choice; either to serve God wholly and exclusively, or else deliberately to choose, and to give oneself to, some other loyalty. This, too, is an issue which requires a decision which is personal, independent, all-embracing. Here we see Joshua re-affirming his own choice, irrespective of what others may decide; and declaring that the decision is to determine the whole ordering of his home and family life. 'But as for me and my household, we will serve the Lord.'

3. *The debt to be remembered.* Read verses 16–18. Provoked by the challenge to choose some other god to serve, the people reply that to abandon their own God in this way, and to serve another, is unthinkable. For they owe their deliverance from bondage, their preservation through danger, and their possession of their inheritance, all to God's doing. Has He not graciously owned them as His people? Is He not openly and unmistakably their God? How can they possibly choose to serve some other god? Our circumstances, too, and therefore our answer, may well be similar. Thinking of ourselves are we not similarly conscious of our debt to God's providence and grace? Have we not often thanked God for our preservation, and, above all, for our redemption? Surely for us to choose now to worship and serve some other god is unthinkable? So, like the Israelites, we too answer: we intend to do as we have long done, and to serve the Lord; for *He is our God.*

4. *The dues to be paid.* Read verses 19 to 23. This profession provoked Joshua to declare that God's service is much more exacting than the Israelites realized. For He is a holy and a jealous God. His service demands clear-cut separation from sin, and exclusive devotion to Him. A declared intention to serve God, such as the Israelites reiterated, is incomplete and unsatisfying, unless it is accompanied by active renunciation of idolatry, and the redirection of the life towards God. They must put away the strange gods which are among them, and incline their hearts to the Lord. And so, too, must we. For this is still the real issue. This is the reason why this kind of challenge still needs to be renewed – to awaken us to the realization that, if the service of God is our choice, we ought to be fully committed to His service. We ought to give up

interests that conflict with the service of God, and set ourselves to love God and delight to do His will. Only so will our Christianity become truly pleasing to God and effective among our neighbours, when we cut out loyalties, devotions, confidences, idolatries, which are inconsistent; and when we actively follow after holiness, by setting ourselves to do what God demands.

5. *The dedication to be covenanted.* Read verses 24, 25. This kind of response is so demanding, so decisive, so determinative of the whole future, which it is customary for it to be solemnly covenanted. This is the reason in society for the solemn public confirmation of the marriage contract – 'forsaking all other, (to) keep thee only unto him, so long as ye both shall live'. This, too, is the reason in the church for the answers to be given, and the vows made, whether in baptism or confirmation. Those who choose to embrace the invitation of the gospel of Christ, and by grace to become the Lord's, thus solemnly pledge their determination to be His alone. Also, attendance at the Holy Communion, particularly when there is put into our hands the cup of the new covenant in Christ's blood, provides opportunity for us frequently to renew our covenant with God, and to pledge afresh our genuine, undivided, life-long devotion.

(vii) *The Conclusion.* So let us solemnly affirm: 'The Lord our God will we serve, and his voice will we obey'; or, still more individually and personally, 'As for me and my household, we will serve the Lord.'

c. The cultivation and expression of true worship (Psalm 95)

NOTE: The psalm here selected for treatment is simple and to some very familiar. Yet it is these very characteristics which cause some great passages to go largely unappreciated. They are never closely studied, phrase by phrase, to discover exactly what they do say. To prepare to expound such a passage one must come to it with a fresh, questioning mind, so to speak, interrogating each sentence, each phrase and sometimes each word in order to register, and preferably to write down, what it expresses, suggests or implies. Any ideas which emerge from this enquiry, which clearly belong together, should be so collected and considered. Equipped with this enriched awareness of detailed content, the would-be expositor should then, as it were, stand back to view the passage as a whole, and possibly to read it aloud to himself more than once, in order to feel the sequence and the coherence and the cumulative force of the whole. In this way he should be in a position to decide what is its dominant theme, and what is the direction of the main thrust of its expression or appeal. He should also be able to see better what points need to be developed, and how. He may therefore lead hearers through the contemplation of the passage both into a fuller appreciation of what God has to say through it, and into a more understanding and deliberate personal response towards God, because of its guidance and challenge. In this way may the preacher combine teaching and exhortation.

EXPOSITION: To regular users of the Book of Common Prayer the words of the *Venite* are very familiar. Just for that reason it is good for us deliberately to pause and consider its contents in order to appreciate the remarkable guidance and help that it gives toward the cultivation and expression of a right spirit of worship. Open a Bible at Psalm 95, and let us pay detailed attention to the wording of each one of the verses.

(i) *The character of worship here in view.* We read 'let us'. This worship is *corporate* – something a number of people do together, something they call upon one another to do. It involves, therefore, a coming together of a congregation. This worship is *vocal*. We read 'let us sing', 'let us make a joyful noise'. Psalms and hymns and their musical accompaniment are to have their place in it. This worship is also to include *actions* that express reverence, submission, and adoration. We are to 'bow down' and to 'kneel'. These, too, are things in which we are all invited deliberately and intelligently and with due preparation to take our share. 'O come, let us worship.'

(ii) *The conditions of its true expression.* Such worship is not to be cultivated and practised directly, just by paying attention to it. For it does not start or end with itself. We have, therefore, to learn to recognize and concentrate attention on two other things without which true worship cannot come to life. These are first, what lies beyond worship, and second, what lies beneath it.

1. *Its goal or purpose.* It is 'before him' and 'to the Lord'. Its end is to honour God not to please self. Its character and content should be determined not by what we desire, but by what He deserves. It is a question not of what I can get out of it, but of what is due to Him in it. Those who come to worship come to give – to God.

2. *Its source and inspiration.* This is, or should be, our personal experience and thankful recollection of God's salvation, of what we owe to His providence and mercy. We are invited to 'come before him with thanks-giving', and to 'let us shout aloud to the Rock of our salvation'. In other words, such worship begins when we count our blessings. Also, in case we forget,

we are clearly meant to stir up one another to come and join in corporate acts of public worship. This surely is an invitation to be extended to our families, friends and neighbours.

(iii) *The way of its expression*. In the activity of worship our one aim should be to acknowledge God and His worthiness. This psalm prompts us to do this in two ways.

1. *We acknowledge God as the sovereign Lord of the universe, as its Creator, Sustainer and King*. So we sing that He made the sea, and His hands formed the dry land. Also, all things are 'in his hand' and under His control. The created order comes from Him and belongs to Him. He is the 'great King', far above all possible rivals. He reigns omnipotent. It is 'to him' we are to sing.

2. *We acknowledge God as the covenant Lord of His people, as their Saviour and Shepherd*. Just as God made the Israelites into a nation and made them His people by redeeming them from Egypt, so Christ by His death for us has made us His; and by the same witness we know that in a new, special, intimate way He is ours. So in awe and adoring wonder we are invited, as those saved by grace and made children of God, to 'kneel before the LORD our maker'. 'For he is *our* God.' Also, as His people, we come directly under His personal care. He is our Shepherd. He looks after us and supplies our needs Himself. We can count on His hand to guide, to provide, to protect, to uphold. So, still overwhelmed with wonder, we go on in adoring worship to confess that 'we are the people of his pasture, the flock under his care'.

(iv) *Its accompanying opportunity and danger.* Worship leads always to a crowning wonder. If we draw near to sing to the Lord we may be quite sure that, as the living God of grace, He will afresh 'today' speak to us through His Word. It is, therefore, all important that we should prepare ourselves to hear and to pay attention to His voice. For even in the place and practice of worship there is a dire personal danger – in case we harden our hearts. So an urgent warning is given, and enforced by reference in some detail to the solemn example of the failure of the Israelites in the wilderness. For before his presence and in the hearing of His Word it is impossible to be neutral. We must either respond or resist, submit or rebel. We cannot be exactly what we were, or where we were, before we came to worship. Before the fresh challenge of His Word our necks either bend or stiffen. Such reaction and result, first in our hearts and then in our ways, are the final test and proof of the sincerity and truth of our psalm singing and our attendance at corporate worship. Finally, how stirring and sobering is the challenge of such a psalm, set as it is in the Prayer Book at the gateway of morning worship for each fresh 'Today'. May the Lord give us grace ever more faithfully to respond to its invitations and to pay attention to its warning.

d. God-given purity and power (Zechariah 3 and 4)

NOTE: There are passages in the Bible which, however obviously they may express or pointedly illustrate some aspect of truth, may with some justice seem insufficient by themselves to provide the preacher with a full theme. It is nevertheless sometimes possible to embrace and use their particular contribution by interpreting them as part of a larger whole. So, in this instance, we may see that justification for studying a longer section (in this case two chapters at once), and occasion for the relatively unusual practice of selecting two 'short texts' to summarize two leading ideas, are alike found in the discovery that truths actually alongside each other in the Bible are in deeper ways theologically and experimentally complementary.

Also, in this case, since the two chapters are in the Old Testament, the message which the Christian preacher may rightly find suggested by them, or which he should use them to present, is only completed and made fully explicit by some reference to the New Testament. The preacher therefore has opportunity to show that the truth latent in the Old Testament is patent in the New Testament; and that what the ancient prophetic words suggest as possible is for the believer in the gospel made present and actual in Christ and by the Spirit.

EXPOSITION: We shall take two short texts for a twofold theme. First, 'See, I have taken away your sin, and I will put rich garments on you.' (3:4). Second, 'Not by might nor by power, but by my Spirit,' says the LORD Almighty' (4:6).

Two things which repeatedly tell against us in the service of God, which we long more worthily to do, are that we are unfit to stand before God and unable to stand before our neighbours. We find ourselves faced in our own lives both by defilement and defeat. We may even be moved to cry: 'Woe is me! for I am undone. This service is too much for me.'

Turn to Zechariah 3 and 4. In the pictures of God's ways, and in the accompanying explanations here given to the ancient prophet of God both to see and to hear, we may in principle discern for our own learning and encouragement God's decisive answers to our own deep personal and practical needs as His servants.

(i) *The way of acceptance before God*. 'He showed me Joshua . . . standing before . . . the LORD' (3:1). This means that Joshua was engaged upon divine service. For 'to stand before' a person, or 'in his presence', is in Hebrew a phrase used to describe the relation of a servant to his master. In Deuteronomy 10:8 we read that 'the Lord separated the tribe of Levi . . . to stand before the Lord to minister unto him'. It was right here, when Joshua was engaged in such sacred service, that the adversary appeared to oppose him, to demand his removal. Since Joshua was clothed in filthy garments, he could not himself refute such an accusation. But the angel of the Lord intervened, and 'stood by' Joshua to serve him. So Joshua was clothed with fair garments, and assured of full freedom of access and participation in service. 'This is what the LORD Almighty says . . . you will govern my house and have charge of my courts, and I will give you a place among these standing here.' (3:7).

Such is the wonder of divine grace. It is the Lord Himself who makes us fit for His presence and His service. 'Listen,' says the Lord of hosts, 'I will am going to bring my servant, the Branch' (3:8). Indeed, only as He thus stands by to serve us can we acquire the fitness to stand and serve Him. Or, as our Lord Himself said to Peter when He became his servant, and stooped to wash his feet, 'Unless I wash you, you have no part with me' (John 13:8).

(ii) *The way of effectiveness before men*. In Zechariah 4 we are given the picture of a candlestick and two olive trees. These both alike find their fulfilment in the possession of oil. Without oil the lamps cannot shine. Without oil the trees will not flourish. The special lesson of this vision is found in the unique way in which these desirable goals are reached, not by natural supplies of oil from below but by special and supernatural supplies from above. There is significantly a bowl upon the top of the candle-stick. From that bowl first the lamps, and then the trees, are supplied with oil; see verses 2, 11 and 12.

The corresponding spiritual truths are also indicated. First, the way of achievement is not by human might, nor by natural power, but by the divine Spirit. 'This is', for God's servant, 'the word of the LORD' (see verse 6). So make no mistake; do not be deceived by the superfi-cial attractiveness of deceptive earthly alternatives. The one way to get the work done is by God's Spirit.

Second, this grace is first to be poured upon the head-stone of the corner (verse 7). For, to change the metaphor, in the Lord's temple the headstone of the cor-ner is the Lord's anointed. It is to Him that the oil of the Spirit is first given without measure. It is from Him, exalted as the Head over the church, that the oil of the Spirit must be received by all who would shine and flourish in God's service on earth. In this way may we, too, become the Lord's 'anointed' (verse 14). Only when the Lord Himself thus upholds us with His power from on high, can we uphold His cause in the high places of the field.

(iii) *The essence of the gospel* is thus here anticipated, and its distinctive benefits indicated. God the Son, by His active intervention as Jehovah's Servant, has put away iniquity in the one decisive day of His finished work of atonement at Calvary. So, as the elect stone of God's lay-ing, He can cause iniquity to pass from us; and we can be made, indeed as His people by grace we are already made, 'the righteousness of God' 'in him' (2 Cor. 5:21).

So we have acceptance before God; we may do Him service. Then, thus accepted by God in Christ, we share the anointing of the chief cornerstone, the Lord's anointed. God the Spirit, by His descent from the exalted Lord, brings into our lives grace, light and strength. This gives us in life and service effectiveness before others. So God meets our need by giving us Himself. God the Son is our God-given purity. God the Spirit is our God-given power.

e. Our world and God's Word (Matthew 24:35–44)

NOTE: This instance provides an instructive and most significant illustration of the importance of expounding a biblical statement not in detached isolation, but in its context, and as part of its context. For here we find not only that God said, 'Heaven and earth will pass away, but my words will never pass away', but also that features of this inevitable crisis of the dissolution of the created order are indicated in what He then went on to say. Also, the complementary implication is that it is in relation to this prospect of the end of the world that the infallibility of Christ's words is of particular relevance. For His words provide the one sure confidence in an insecure world; and they give us, as people who have to face a future of complete uncertainty, awareness of things which are certain of fulfilment. So the faithful expositor of the whole passage should make plain that what adds to the practical value of God's Word is the prospect of inevitable dissolution which confronts our present world.

Here, too, we may learn from the practice of Jesus Himself how to use and apply the witness of the Old Testament to illustrate and to enforce truths supremely fulfilled in the New Testament and at the coming of the Son of man.

EXPOSITION: This passage of our Lord's own teaching challenges us, if we will pay attention to it, to recognize the unique character, the supreme worth and the abiding practical value of the Word of God. Reference to it is here put in the context of the advent and eschatology, in relation, that is, to the future coming of Christ and the end of the world. That is the right setting in which to appreciate its outstanding worth. For in this setting the Word of God is seen to be our one security in a completely insecure world. 'Heaven and earth', said Jesus, 'will pass away, but my words will never pass away' (verse 35, the 'short text' for the exposition).

(i) *A pertinent contrast.* The certainty of God's Word to endure, to continue to hold good, and to find fulfilment, is set in contrast with the insecurity of the natural order of 'heaven and earth', in which we think there is stability and permanence. For men and women of a scientific age like ours sometimes tend to talk as if the laws of the natural order were the one thing that cannot be broken. They have little or no respect for words of professed divine revelation, and particularly for words of predictive prophecy. Indeed they sometimes fondly imagine that they can rightly treat them with the incredulity which they suppose they deserve. We do well to set in radical contrast with such ideas these significant words of Jesus: 'Heaven and earth will pass away, but my words will never pass away.'

(ii) *A pointed comparison.* 'As it was in the days of Noah, so it will be at the coming of the Son of Man' (verse 37). The story of the flood and of what happened before it came is, said Jesus Himself, an illustration of conditions which will recur before the predicted end of the world comes and the Son of man appears. In this story of the days of Noah we may discern the same contrasts. First, there is the contrast between the mistaken attitude of humans both to their own world and to God's Word and the actual truth. Second, there is the contrast between the unrecognized insecurity of the world of the human race and the unbelieved certainty of God's Word. In those days the world carried on as usual, absorbed in its own immediate interests, supposing that its life was stable and enduring. Nor did it apparently give any scientifically observable indication of the impending destruction. Over against this was a God-given word of clear and solemn warning. But this word people treated with incredulity and indifference. 'They knew nothing about what would happen until the flood came and took them all away', said Jesus. 'That is how it will be at the coming of the Son of Man.' (verse 39).

(iii) *A paradoxical crisis*. In the days of Noah with over-whelming suddenness and completeness 'the flood came, and took them all away'. This decisively exposed the real truth. Humankind's world was shown to be completely insecure. God's Word was shown to be absolutely certain. The same crisis paradoxically overthrew the one and vindicated the other. The truth of God's Word and the doom of man's world were alike thrown into stark relief. It was impossible any longer to disbelieve or refute either. The one event served conclusively to demonstrate both human beings' folly and God's faithfulness.

(iv) *Our prospect comparable*. It is Jesus who said that this is an exact picture of the kind of thing which will happen again at His second coming. The final catastrophe of judgment will both destroy the world and fulfil His Word. Heaven and earth are to pass away. Christ's words are to abide and to find fulfilment. With dramatic suddenness men and women will find themselves divided; one taken and the other left; one saved and the other lost. Nor is any knowledge of the actual day possible. We simply have Christ's own word that He is coming.

(v) *The practical challenge.* This surely is plain enough. We need to beware in case we too be deceived by the prevailing worldly attitude and outlook of our neighbours. We need to gain a proper perspective, a true sense of values. To do so we ought above all else to prize the God-given Word. We ought to pay attention to its warning, to enjoy its comfort, to embrace and hold fast its hope. We ought to expect and to anticipate its fulfilment. 'Our Lord, come!' (1 Cor. 16:22, ESV). So said Christ, 'keep watch' (verse 42). 'So you also must be ready' (verse 44).

f. The blessings of the new covenant (Hebrews 7:10–12)

NOTE: We are here to consider an outstanding scriptural statement. It occurs in the first place in Jeremiah 31; and it has been said with some justification to be the greatest promise of the Old Testament Scriptures. In quoting it the writer to the Hebrews is indicating that these are the blessings now to be enjoyed in Christ. Yet the length and solid substance of this statement tend to frighten off preachers; and so its exposition is not attempted, and God's people are not instructed as they should be concerning the spiritual privileges that are made theirs in the new covenant of the gospel. The passage is, therefore, here included and expounded as an illustration of the kind of solid doctrinal statement that preachers and teachers of God's Word ought more frequently and more fully to expound.

Also, this exposition happens to provide occasion to suggest that sometimes people may be led step by step into a fuller grasp of a passage as a whole by treating its details in reverse order, or in an order different from the one in which they are ultimately and (to the now appreciative mind) understandably set forth in the written Word of God.

EXPOSITION: By the words of Jesus at its institution the service of Holy Communion is explicitly connected with the new covenant – a covenant sealed by the shed blood of Christ Himself. In this service He invites us to appropriate our share in the covenant, to eat and to drink as those called by divine grace to enjoy privileges and benefits, which are not only made ours by Christ's death, but are also sealed to us as ours by these visible covenant pledges, of which we are invited to partake. That we may use this service the more profitably let us then remind ourselves what these blessings are, and thus prepare ourselves the more consciously and deliberately to embrace them, by turning our thoughts to consider the actual terms and specific promises of God's new covenant. Let us not forget either that if we wish to be, and to continue to be, 'evangelical', in the proper sense of the word, it is this heritage of the gospel, or new covenant, which we need to embrace, and to which we ought to hold fast. For one of the surprising dangers which has persisted in the church ever since the beginning is that people who begin by embracing the new covenant, should then slip back into the pattern and bondage of the old.

Let us then read the terms of the new covenant in Hebrews 8:10–12. This statement, it would seem, is best appreciated if we regard it as starting, so to speak, at the coping-stone and working downwards to the foundation. In order, therefore, to appreciate how the fullness of gospel blessing is built up let us here consider the points mentioned in reverse order.

(i) *Sin forgiven and forgotten* (verse 12). This is the initial or foundation blessing – the remission and complete removal of sin. The distinctive gospel experience begins here in the complete putting away of sin. This means realized peace with God. It is the sure and sufficient ground of full assurance – assurance that there is from this point on no condemnation. This brings release from uncertainty and endless sacrifice. There is no further need or place for sin-offering (see Hebrews 10:18). We can simply rest and rejoice in 'the finished work of Christ'.

(ii) *Intimate personal knowledge of God as an experience to be enjoyed direct by every single individual* (verse 11). This means, in other words – and words which enshrine yet more of our evangelical treasure – direct access to the full intimacy of God's presence through Christ alone for all alike, with no dependence upon any mediating human priests. It also means in implied consequence the right of private judgment – that is, the ability of every believer to speak with the awareness of direct personal insight into the things of God. Above all, it means that all alike know Him, whom to know is life eternal.

(iii) *The consciousness of being one of the Lord's own chosen people* (verse 10c). For this we have the Lord's own explicit promise: 'I will be their God, and they will be my people.' This means that our relation to God is no empty form, no mere outward profession or nominal adherence, but vital personal union. Like a newly-married woman speaking of her husband, the believer can say of his Lord, 'I am His, and He is mine.' This awareness alters everything. 'Heaven above is softer blue, earth around is sweeter green.' 'Things that once were wild alarms cannot now disturb my rest.' And why? – 'since I know, as now I know, I am His and He is mine'.

(iv) *Inner transformation of heart desire caused by the indwelling Spirit* (verse 10). 'I will put my laws in their minds and write them on their hearts.' The complement of my intimacy with Him is His indwelling and working in me. This means a radical change of heart desire, so that I begin to say, 'I delight to do your will' (see Psalm 40:8). In other words, God works in us to will and to do (Phil. 2:13). A new life becomes possible and certain, not by submitting to external restraint, nor by keeping a hundred and one rules, but by reason of an inner constraint making us delight to do God's will. Such service is perfect freedom. So may God make us perfect in every good thing to do His will, working in us that which is well-pleasing in His sight, through Jesus Christ; to whom be the glory for ever and ever. Amen. (See Hebrews 13:20,21.)

Obeying God's Word

The call to true discipleship

Contents

Preface

There is a tendency today for students of the Bible to be too exclusively intellectual and theoretical in their approach, too detached, too absorbed in the scientific investigation of how it was written, and what it meant to its first writers and readers. The danger is that we grow only in critical knowledge of the Bible, instead of, through its use, growing in knowledge of God and in obedience to His will. For, as a divinely provided handbook for our use, it is intended by God to promote knowledge of Him, understanding of His ways, enjoyment of His grace and salvation, and active co-operation in doing His will. The practical demands which the Bible makes on its readers are, therefore, spiritual and moral. It invites the response of faith and obedience to our Father, of reverence and right living. We need, therefore, pointedly to ask ourselves whether we have adequately faced up in this way to the practical authority of the Word of God as something which should determine what we believe, what we teach, and how we act. The simple purpose of this book is to use the witness and exposition of the Scriptures themselves to press home this challenge.

Alan Stibbs

Important note: To read this book with full understanding and benefit it is best to do so alongside an open Bible – continually read or consult the many passages mentioned and expounded.

1

The Importance of Obedience

1. The implications of biblical inspiration

Our acknowledgement of the divine inspiration of the Bible is of great practical importance to us as Christians because of the function which God intends that its proper use should fulfil in our lives. This function is nowhere more decisively indicated than in the words from the Old Testament (actually Deut. 8:3), which Jesus quoted as His first answer to the temptations of the devil. He said, 'It is written: "Man does not live on bread alone, but on every word that comes from the mouth of God."' (Matt. 4:4; cf. Luke 4:4.)

Other animals live by food; that is enough for them. But humans are unique. We cannot truly live by bread alone. For us life is to be found only in conscious dependence on God, and in sustained devotion to God. It is to inspire and to inform these essential activities that the God-inspired Word has been given.

The written Word of God is therefore of direct practical value for human living for two main reasons. First, it tells us what God is doing, or is willing to do. It reveals His purposes. It is a book of prophecies and promises. Second, it tells us what we ought to do in order to please

God, and to share in the benefits of His activity; it also warns us what not to do if we are to avoid wrongdoing and escape God's condemnation. It is a book both of precepts and of actual or virtual prohibitions.

The true way to enjoy life is to trust and obey; on the one hand, to count wholly on God's doing, and, on the other hand, to contribute one's own doing. Guidance for practising such a twofold response to God is to be found in the Bible. It is the one authoritative textbook of faith and conduct for Christians.

From the Bible, then, as a handbook of the faith, we may learn what God is like, and what He has done; we may learn about the Saviour whom He sent, and gain informed conviction concerning His Person and His work; we may learn how salvation can be made ours, and worked out in our daily lives by the indwelling Spirit; and we may learn how all these purposes of God's saving grace are to be consummated in the great coming day of the Lord, when the Saviour will reappear and gather around Him His glorified people. All this and more of God's revealed truth we ought to know, believe, embrace and propagate. Nor can we fully enjoy and declare our faith and hope as Christians except by a detailed knowledge and understanding of all the Bible teaches. So we ought to be diligent and prayerful students of God's Word.

The Bible is also a handbook of conduct. By its aid and instruction we are meant to learn moral discernment and so be able to discern between good and evil, so that we may actively choose the good and refuse the evil. If, therefore, we are to order our lives as we ought as children of God, we need continually to put ourselves under the instruction and correction of God's written Word, and thus let our wrong actions be exposed and condemned, and our right actions determined and approved, by its plain and pointed precepts, and by the application of its principles.

Christ commissioned His followers not only to preach the gospel, which they had only to believe in order to be saved, but also to teach converts to observe all the things which He had commanded. This is still our plain Christian obligation. Nor can we thus lead others into truths which we do not ourselves both believe and practise. Living the Christian life properly demands, therefore, daily and detailed attention to what the Bible says. It demands not only a spirit of faith in God's promises, but also a sensitive conscience about obeying His precepts. Indeed, there is in the New Testament explicit warning that those who think they can hold fast to the faith without such conscientious obedience will become spiritual shipwrecks.

We rightly acknowledge the Bible to be God's own inspired Word, because we believe that such assent is indispensable to true spiritual well-being. But soundness in the faith will not be preserved or fully guaranteed simply by signing a doctrinal basis, important as that is. For to be 'sound' in the faith means to be healthy or spiritually fit as a Christian believer. Such health is morally conditioned. We must be doers of the Word and not believers only. So we should, by our diligent and prayer-soaked daily study of the Bible, first let our faith be inspired and informed, and then allow our conduct to be tested and directed, by plain, detailed and biblical teaching. For this is the only way properly to confirm our confession of the divine inspiration of the Bible – by consistent and conscientious use of it as our rule of faith and conduct.

2. Exposition of Psalm 119:1–24, 33–35

It seems wise to confirm these general statements by some detailed exposition of an actual Bible passage. One obviously directly relevant to our subject is Psalm 119.

John Ruskin wrote of this psalm that it 'has become of all the most precious to me in its overflowing and glorious passion of love for the law of God'. To appreciate it one needs to have in one's own heart and life the spirit and aspirations of the psalmist. Since this is equally true of the appreciation of the subject of this whole book, we do well to pray fervently for the God-given increase in us of this spirit. The psalmist's words may excite our interest and help to direct our desires in prayer. Let us look then (with a Bible open) at the first two or three stanzas of Psalm 119.

Verses 1–8 speak of the blessedness of those who unfailingly observe God's law. The comprehensive embrace and the diverse character of God's Word are here expressed by a suggestive variety of descriptive names – His testimonies and His ways, His precepts and His laws, His commandments and His righteous judgments or decrees – all related to the varied circumstances and needs of human living. The practical and all-absorbing nature of our consequent responsibility to obey – to make the only adequate response of obedience – is unmistakably indicated by such words as 'walk', 'keep' and 'do'. What is more, such response is to be made 'diligently' and 'with the whole heart' – with full concentration of mind and will. It involves having respect for God's commandments, paying attention to them with the deliberate intention of acting accordingly, learning with a view to doing. This is the consuming passion of the psalmist's life. 'Oh, that my ways were steadfast in obeying your decrees!' What is thus stirred in him – and it is important to see this clearly – is not some devotion to the impersonal law (what some would call bibliolatry), but an outgoing of spirit in worship, prayer and desire towards God Himself. Through keeping His commandments, the psalmist expects to find God, to be without shame in His presence, and to delight in His praise. So let us learn that the whole purpose of our response to God's Word in faith and obedience is to fulfil our chief aim, which is 'to glorify God and to enjoy Him for ever'.

Verses 9–16 indicate the way of moral purity, of keeping clean, of avoiding evil, of realizing the highest aspirations of youth. On the one hand, one must be prepared to recognize the essential character of disobedience as impurity or spoiling, as wandering or turning from the divinely indicated right way to the self-willed wrong way, and, above all, as sinning against God and directly displeasing Him. On the other hand, one needs to realize how right standards of behaviour are learnt and practised by acting according to God's Word, by bringing one's actions daily into the light and under the judgment of the Word of God; by seeking God with one's whole heart, by being so absorbed with pleasing Him so as to be saved from wandering and waywardness; and by hiding God's Word in one's heart, or storing it in one's memory, so as to be able to recollect it and to use it to detect the beginnings of sin, and openly to delight in ways pleasing to God.

In verses 17–24 the psalmist confesses his desire for, and his delight in, the discovery and the doing of the will of God. To him the very purpose and satisfaction of life itself is to keep God's Word. His great need, his urgent prayer, is as a willing learner to understand God's law that it may illuminate his darkness and inform his ignorance. This is with him an all-consuming passion, and the more so because he knows that the only alternative to this way of humility, obedience and blessing is the way of pride and error.

This urgent request for understanding with a view to obedience is particularly repeated in Psalm 119:33–35. Such words ought to make us all examine ourselves to see whether we have the same practical end of obedience in view in all our Bible study. Also, the psalmist here teaches us by practice rather than by precept, that the beginnings of right response to this very challenge are to be found in praying as he did

> Teach me, O LORD, to follow your decrees; then I will keep them to the end. Give me understanding, and I will keep your law and obey it with all my heart. Direct me in the path of your commands, for there I find delight.

2

Temptation and Defeat

The story of the fall of the human race into sin is a story of our failure to maintain practical, unquestioning obedience to the God-given Word. Let us turn to the story, as it is recorded in Genesis 3:1–6. But first we must note that Adam, as a new creature in a new world, needed, and was given, some plain instructions that he might know how to act both to please God, and to promote his own well-being. What he was given was words from God – words of authority and revelation, words of objective truth and direct practical importance, disclosing for his information and benefit facts of which he would otherwise have been ignorant. 'And the LORD God commanded the man, "You are free to eat from any tree in the garden; but you must not eat from the tree of the knowledge of good and evil, for when you eat of it you will surely die"' (Gen. 2:16,17). These clear directions combined both permission and pro-hibition. They gave both positive guidance and negative warning. They demanded and deserved unquestioning acceptance and uncompromising obedience. Adam's safety depended upon their diligent observance. He was thus challenged in his own interests to become a doer of God's Word. This was then, and still is, our chief responsi-bility – to become a doer of God's Word.

Then came the devil and immediately began to seek to divert Adam and Eve from the pathway of obedience, and to do it by a campaign of words. He brought to the task not over-powering armaments but specious arguments. His first utterance ended with a question mark. This is how misleading propaganda commonly begins; that is, by seeking to raise doubts about things which one thought one could take for granted. Such questioning was extremely subtle; for it sought to undermine their confidence in the one foundation on which alone they could stand secure. The one sufficient reason why Eve should have been determined to abide by the divine command was simply because God had said it. The serpent, therefore, attacked the authorship of the command as the sure way to undermine its authority. He asked, 'Did God really say . . . ?' He raised questions such as, Are you quite sure *God* did say it? Or can He have *meant* exactly what you thought He meant? Surely it is inconceivable that a loving Creator should restrict the freedom of His creatures? And all the time the devil's motive was not to promote a better understanding of the mind of God, but to persuade Eve to disown the one expression of His mind which she did possess; and therefore to make herself into a creature without any authoritative guidance, and consequently one ready to be misled by cleverly designed suggestions. In other words, the devil was out to break down her defences and to make her open to invasion by foreign ideas. His method of achieving this was the more deadly because apparently so harmless. What harm could there be in indulging in a little speculation about the trees of the garden? Yet the truth was that once Eve entertained the subject as one open to question at all, she had taken the first step towards capitulation; for she had given a dangerous enemy a menacing foothold inside her own mind.

Having in this way obtained a foothold within Eve's mind by his questioning, the serpent at once pressed home the attack. The first stage had been to entice Eve to abandon the attitude of submissive acceptance of the divine Word, simply because it was God's Word, and to lead her to face the question on her own from her own observation of the facts. The second stage consisted in encouraging still greater presumption. He now enticed Eve to adopt an attitude of superiority, to sit in judgment on the facts, to come to her own conclusion, and actually to decide against, and to reject, the Word of God, and to dare to deny or contradict it. 'You will not surely die'; surely so serious a consequence as death would not follow from the simple act of eating? The third stage completed the conquest. The devil now invited Eve to active independence and open rebellion. He called for the full outburst of self-assertion. He appealed wholly to selfish pride. He actually suggested that the prohibition was designed to keep them out of something good, to hold them in bondage. 'For God knows that when you eat of it your eyes will be opened, and you will be like God, knowing good and evil.' One twentieth-century way of putting this is that religion is dope for the masses, something that we must reject if we are ever to be free and find fulfilment. So the devil called, as he still calls, for open rebellion, for proud presumption, for defiant ungodliness – and all by the subtlety of misleading words.

Nor was such enticement unsuccessful; Eve responded and disobeyed the divine command. Nor are similar arguments any less successful today; for it is by the same three stages that many are still deceived into departing from God's Word. First, they depart in thought and begin to doubt the authority of the Bible, then they depart in word and do not hesitate to deny the truth of the Bible, and finally they depart in deed, and act in disobedience and even in deliberate defiance of the plain instructions of the Bible. All that the words of divine command can now do for those people is to demonstrate that they are sinners. 'Through the law we become conscious of sin' (Rom. 3:20).

There is a further question which is worthy of some detailed consideration. We have seen how the devil advanced in his attack on Eve. 'We are?,' as St Paul says, 'not ignorant of his devices' (2 Cor. 2:11). It is valuable to try to see why Eve surrendered. What from her point of view were the grounds of her decision and consequent action? What persuaded her to alter her mind and to abandon God's way? The answer is that there were two inducements, one from outside, the other from inside; first the serpent's suggestions, and second her own feelings and conclusions; in other words, the devil and self. She allowed these to take the place in her mind of God and His Word.

This means, in the first place, that she ceased to look up for guidance. She tried to take her bearings and to steer her course solely by local evidence, solely by the help of voices without and within, instead of by the light of God-given revelation.

What is more, it means, in the second place, that she rejected the authoritative instructions of her best friend (the Creator, who made the trees, and to whom she owed everything, i.e. the One most likely to know) for the unsupported assertion of an unknown stranger. Nor are people today any different. We are still led astray in this way. Let us learn from Eve's mistakes to beware of approaches whose chief aim is to persuade us to abandon the best in order to follow the latest.

In the third place, Eve depended on sense observation and inner feeling. She pitted her own subjective fancy against the God-given objective fact. She used the supposed findings of natural science and psychology to oppose the plain witness of theology. God had said that to eat of this particular tree would be fatal. Eve preferred to go by her own feelings and her independent judgment. It looked pleasant. Surely such attractive-looking fruit must be good for food? In addition, the serpent said it would do her good, and that she would be the loser if she refrained from eating. So the strong and irrepressible desire to eat was awakened; and this mere sensual yearning or physical appetite won the day. Eve became a victim of misdirected instincts. Having already yielded to ungodliness she now yielded to worldly lusts. (See Titus 2:12.)

In the fourth place, Eve was deceived by specious rationalization – by arguments and an explanation which all seemed to justify eating. The command not to eat, because to do so would be fatal, was represented by the devil, and slowly and surely regarded by Eve herself, as unworthy of God, unsupported by the evidence, and unfair on the humans involved. Consequently it was disowned as a guide to action. Eve's conscience and her innate reverence for the Word of God were overpowered and their witness silenced by the breaking down of facts and the bolstering up of imagination by specious arguments. The serpent could not of course alter the objective truth of the Word, that to eat would be fatal, but he could and did persuade Eve to alter the subjective attitude of her mind, so that she now believed that to eat would be beneficial. In other words, he persuaded her, as he still seeks to persuade us, to use reason to criticize and deny revelation, and thus to justify departure from the Word of God.

The consequence was that Eve was doubly deceived. She was enticed into choosing a false way to obtain a desired good at the cost of forsaking the true way to avoid actual evil. She couldn't have been saved from such a fatal step except by steadfast adherence to the God-given Word. For she could herself experimentally discover whether all her theorizing about the tree was correct or not only by actually eating the fruit. And then, if her theorizing were wrong, it would be too late to avoid the consequent damage.

For example, if you found a bottle of strange liquid plainly marked 'poison', if a bystander asserted it was not poison but a refreshing drink, and if you removed the cork and were attracted by the smell, no matter how thirsty you were, you would still, and wisely, be inclined to give the label the benefit of the doubt, and to refrain from experimental drinking. Too much would be at stake if you drank, only to find that the label was right after all!

Similarly the statements of divine revelation deal with facts outside our power to prove or disprove by logical argument. Too much is at stake for us lightly to disregard them. Even from the standpoint of prudent self-interest they deserve to be given the benefit of the doubt, in case they may be true. And when we consider their established and enduring authority, and the testimony of the thousands who have found their happiness in obeying them, it is even more obvious that our only wisdom, and indeed our only safety, is to live by them.

It is, therefore, a tragedy of infinite seriousness when misleading propaganda and presumptuous speculation cause us to inflict eternal damage upon ourselves, to disbelieve and to depart from God's Word, and sometimes openly to deny and even to defy its plain statements and explicit commands. Yet this is where we all have failed and gone astray; leaving the way of God's commandments we have all turned to our own way. Judged by this standard of full obedience to the Word of God we all stand under condemnation and in peril of judgment as sinners.

3

Temptation and Victory

The record of Jesus' temptations in the wilderness is remarkably complementary to the story of Genesis 3; it is its evangelical counterpart. Put together, the two stories show first, how the first Adam failed, and second, how the second Adam prevailed in the encounter with temptation. The devil first encountered the human race in the place where God had put them. Adam and Eve failed in a garden where they lacked nothing. Jesus as Man for men met the devil, by contrast, in a wilderness. He prevailed in the place where He seemed to lack everything. Success or failure, therefore, clearly does not depend on environment. Let us take the account of the temptation given us in Matthew 4 and consider it section by section.

a) Matthew 4:1–4

It is surely significant also that the first man's initial fall into sin and the second Man's decisive victory over temptation both involved facing an appeal to our need of, and appetite for, food. Adam and Eve fell when they ate the fruit of the forbidden tree. Jesus prevailed when, hungry though He was, He refused to make bread to eat.

Temptation, therefore, commonly has to do with appetites which in themselves are physically natural and morally neutral. What the devil does is to strive to exploit, to misdirect, and to degrade fundamentally proper and legitimate desires. Thus bread or food – that is, the very thing which satisfies appetite – becomes a means of enticement or testing. For, although food is a necessity of life, it is not the first necessity. It must be kept in its place as a means not an end. We need to recognize there are higher interests which must be given priority even over satisfying appetite. For the ultimate guarantee of life and its continuance is found not in having food to eat, but in abiding by God's Word and in doing His will. In this pathway of obedience we, as servants of God, are immortal till our work is done. Our lives will undoubtedly be sustained.

So, to the temptation to make bread in order to preserve life, Jesus answered: 'It is written: "Man does not live on bread alone, but on every word that comes from the mouth of God."' Indeed, to each one of the three temptations Jesus answered, 'It is written' and then quoted a plain biblical precept or rule. To every enticement He said in effect that there were certain things which it would be wrong to do, and that what made this absolutely certain was the God-given Word of instruction. Here then we have an outstanding illustration of the supreme value and the practical use of the written Word of God. It provides plain indication of the governing principles of life and liberty, of true safety and well-being. It is, therefore, suicidal not to abide by the God-given Word and to obey its clear instructions.

Our natural consciousness of appetite or hunger and still more the experience of actual shortage of food do not, however, make falling into sin inevitable. Rather they provide opportunity to learn the practical application of life's deeper governing principle. So God in His providence allows men to hunger in order to find out which they will put first – obedience to Him or the satisfaction of appetite. It was, indeed, from a scriptural testimony to this truth, in connection with God's dealings with the Israelites, when they, too, were in the wilderness and hungry, that Jesus quoted when He answered the devil's first temptation. For, in Deuteronomy 8:2,3, it is written

> Remember how the LORD your God led you all the way in the desert these forty years, to humble you and to test you in order to know what was in your heart, whether or not you would keep his commands. He humbled you, causing you to hunger and then feeding you with manna, which neither you nor your fathers had known, to teach you that man does not live on bread alone but on every word that comes from the mouth of the LORD.

So there are times in human experience when for our safety and God's glory we must place the precepts and prohibitions of God's written Word over the pressure of feeling and appetite. For, while humans must eat to live, the first principle of life is not eating, but obedience to the laws which condition the healthy enjoyment of life. For instance, in the matter of marriage and sex too much prominence often tends to be given to natural feelings and desires, and to the satisfaction of appetite or so-called 'love' – what the Bible calls the 'desires of the sinful nature'. What is often forgotten is the overriding sanction of the Word of God. People too readily forget that a successful marriage and healthy and happy family life can be realized only through the proper observance of those strict and sacred laws governing sexual relations, which have been so plainly laid down by our God – the God who instituted marriage. It is from the

God-given Word, and not only from our own human and sometimes sinful and selfish instincts and emotions, that we need to learn how to preserve and to possess the true purity and potential beauty of married life.

One may, in illustration, compare a long distance express train, which has but recently started out on its journey, and is stopped by a signal at 'danger'. While the passengers may all be eager to speed on their way, while the engine may be completely ready to go, it would be wrong for the driver not to stop and wait until the 'all-clear' sign is given. Safety in train driving is secured not by desire to arrive, nor by self-assertive unwillingness to stop or to wait, but by submission to direction. The visible witness, which reveals the condition of the unseen line ahead, deserves prompt and unquestioning obedience. Similarly the God-given Word should govern and restrain all satisfaction of human appetite and all expression of human activity.

b) Matthew 4:5–7

Appetite for food is not, however, the only legitimate human desire which the devil tries to distort. There are also the spirit of adventure and the urge of ambition. For it is in the blood of some to be adventurous, to be daring; and it is a natural and healthy thing to desire to succeed and to win place or power among others. It is these stirrings of desire which give the devil corresponding opportunity to misdirect their expression. So the characteristic elements of the world of sinful humanity include not only 'the desires of the sinful nature', but also 'the lust of his eyes and the boasting of what he has and does'. These are the things which all come to nothing and pass away; for they end in sin and death. In direct opposition to them it is only the man or woman, who by remaining in the Word of God does the will of God. (See 1 John 2:15–17)

The remaining two temptations of the Saviour show how He encountered and answered enticements to misdirect first, the spirit of adventure, and second, the urge of ambition. Let us first consider the former, the temptation to throw Himself down from a pinnacle of the temple. This was a temptation to win applause and acclamation by sensational display. It was an enticement to reckless, unjustified and potentially disastrous venture. Yet it was very subtly and attractively presented. For Jesus had just taken His stand on God's Word and confessed His faith in God's preservation. He had refused to be misled by fearful and unbelieving rationalism. So, by a master in the art of temptation, He was promptly encouraged to engage in an act of reckless and irrational credulity. The devil quoted a word from the Scriptures which promised divine protection. He encouraged Jesus to step out adventurously within His chosen pathway of absolute faith in God and His Word, when actually, to deliberately throw Himself down would have been an act of folly and presumption, a departure from the appointed way of God for His son – a way in which He alone had promised to protect Him. (Note that in quoting Ps. 91:11,12 the devil omitted 'in all your ways'; for this was an enticement deliberately to depart from God's way, and still to expect protection.)

Again Jesus answered by an appeal to first principles, by quoting a plain biblical prohibition: 'Do not put the Lord your God to the test.' Also He deliberately set the restriction imposed by this precept against the encouragement to venture apparently promised in the Bible. He answered, 'It is also written.' And this other verse made it plain that to act in that way would involve failure to maintain a due sense of responsibility for the stewardship of life. It would in fact have been to play the fool and to tempt Providence. One cannot violate a principle and then expect to claim a promise. So the kind of action which the devil suggested was completely ruled out.

Here there is a most important truth for all to learn who are eager to live the life of Christian faith and devotion. For this temptation makes all too plain that, if the devil cannot prevent us from being spiritual and believing, God-conscious and counting on God's promises, he will tempt us extravagantly to overdo such devotion and to lose our heads and misapply some imagined scriptural guidance in some wild venture of so-called faith. It is fatally wrong to suppose that we can force God's hand to work for us by recklessly throwing ourselves down into danger. Rather it is for God's faithful servants to keep God's way, and to wait patiently for Him to lift us up to possess the promised inheritance. (See Ps. 37:5–7,34; John 12:32.)

c) Matthew 4:8–11

The devil's third temptation for Jesus was an appeal to ambition; it was based on His desire to achieve conquest. The devil was not wrong to suppose that the Messiah was out for big things in the world. What he did was to suggest a quick road to success, to tempt Jesus to forsake principle for power, to sell His soul in order to gain the world, only to find if He did that He was serving not the Lord but the devil. Also, this account illustrates as no other can that such temptation does come to one whose motives are unselfish, who is out to do good.

Here Jesus at once sensed the fundamental disloyalty of treason. Such a proposal could come only from the main opponent of God, the ultimate traitor, with whom there can be no possible compromise or discussion. So the Saviour did not engage in argument or discussion with him. He spoke abrupt and decisive words of dismissal, and appealed to the supreme principle, which made any response to such a proposal absolutely unthinkable. 'Jesus said to him, "Away from me, Satan! For it is written: 'Worship the Lord your God, and serve him only.'"'

This, then, is life's primary and exclusive loyalty – to worship the Lord our God, to serve Him only. The one purpose of attending to and observing His Word is to maintain this loyalty unimpaired and to give it suitable expression. So notice that in each one of Jesus' three answers to temptation this conscious Godward relation is fundamental. It is this direct reference to God, to His will, His ways, and His claims, that correctly settles what we may or may not do. Such reference is actually made in explicit relation to life's varying circumstances and frequent temptations, by the recollection, understanding and application of particular Scriptures and the underlying principles shown or displayed there. To avoid being misled by excess of zeal or credulity it is important to preserve the balance of truth by weighing verse against verse. Finally, just as the fear of God is the beginning of right understanding, so His service is the end of all true obedience. His Word deserves and demands active compliance. Ideally we submit gladly and wholeheartedly to its restraints and act under its constraints. Only in this way we can please God and enjoy His blessing. It's only like this that in our present imperfect circumstances can we become 'more than conquerors through him who loved us' (Rom. 8: 37).

4

Obeying the Gospel

1. The principle of the obedience of faith

In the world into which Adam and Eve were put, all things were of God, created by Him to fulfil His will and purpose. Adam and Eve could themselves make nothing new; nor could they alter the character of human life, and make it different by their own independent activity. They were dependent creatures. Their privilege and calling were to find their place and fulfilment in the order of God's creation, by learning His way from His Word, gladly accepting it, and diligently observing it. Disaster occurred because they departed from this obedience of faith in God and His appointed way. They ceased to act on the God-given Word. In other words, the fall of man into sin was due to the disobedience of unbelief.

The Fall brought us under God's condemnation and made us subject to death as the penalty of sin. Our position was now hopeless and helpless, apart from the utterly undeserved intervention of God in redeeming grace. The human race was, in fact, wholly in God's hands as the sovereign Creator and Judge; wholly dependent on His will and His working for all hope of salvation and life. For any redemption from sin and re-establishment in life must of necessity doubly be all of God, entirely His doing. Only if God chose to act, and only if God Himself provided the solution, was there any hope of deliverance.

So human beings, fallen in sin, were thrown back upon the principle they had abandoned, the principle of the obedience of faith in God, as alone affording any hope of salvation. Consequently the gospel to be preached to sinners makes the principle of obedience of faith doubly necessary. Not only is it the principle of enjoying life in fellowship with God, once the sinner regains it; but also it is the only instruction whose practice can bring hope and help to one fallen and doomed in sin. For, if you are to be saved, God must do it, and you must wholly trust God to rescue you. Also, if you are to be saved, God must show the way, and provide the means, and you must submit to the directions, and accept what is given, and become wholly and unquestioningly obedient. Hope dawns, therefore, for the sinner in relation to God and the gospel of saving grace, when he or she recommences the practice of the obedience of faith. To this we must deliberately return.

Not only, therefore, can there be no enjoyment of the blessings of the gospel without faith; but also, there can be no such enjoyment without repentance, whereby the sinner renounces the disobedience of his or her unbelief, and returns to the obedience of faith in God. So Jesus began His public preaching by commanding: 'Repent and believe the good news!' (Mark 1:15). So Paul testified 'to both Jews and Greeks that they must turn to God in repentance and have faith in our Lord Jesus' (Acts 20:21). And he declared that his gospel and 'the proclamation of Jesus Christ' was 'according to the revelation of the mystery,' which is now 'revealed and made known . . . by the command of the eternal God, so that all nations might believe and obey him' (Rom. 16:25,26).

Of this evangelical and saving truth concerning the purpose of God to save, and concerning our way to enjoy the benefit of salvation, the Bible gives many illustrations. They all make plain that we must believe and respond to the God-given Word in the obedience of faith. For 'without faith it is impossible to please God' (Heb. 11:6); and 'faith without deeds is dead' (Jas 2:26).

a) Hebrews 11:7

In the days before the flood Noah's reverence for God and faith in Him made him pay attention to the warning provided by the God-given Word concerning the certain coming judgment of the flood. It also made him act on the guidance provided by God concerning the way to be preserved from drowning. So Noah gave himself to the task of preparing an ark. By this active outgoing of faith in responsive obedience Noah not only himself found acceptance with God; he was also God's instrument for saving his family. In addition, as 'a preacher of righteousness' (2 Pet. 2:5), he was used as a witness to his generation, which served to increase the justice of the condemnation to destruction of the unbelieving and disobedient world.

b) Exodus 11:4–7; 12:3–13

When the Israelites were still in bondage in Egypt, and God was planning to bring them out to be His people, God gave them through Moses plain warning of the impending judgment upon the firstborn of every Egyptian family – and equally plain witness of the way in which His people might find protection against corresponding judgment in their own homes. On the appointed night all the firstborn in the land of Egypt would die; but such destruction would not come to any Israelite house whose door posts had been duly sprinkled with the shed blood of a slaughtered lamb. So said the God-given Word; and the Israelites not only believed it, they acted on it. They believed that God would do what He said; that the judgment would happen; and that divine protection from it would follow, if they made use of it. So in each Israelite home the shed blood was sprinkled; and the firstborn son was saved. And all as an expression and a consequence of the faithfulness of God and of the corresponding obedience of their faith in God.

c) Numbers 21:4–9

Here we read that the Israelites in the wilderness were disturbed, as a judgment from God, by snakes whose bite caused many to die. They acknowledged their sin, and looked for help from God alone. God gave guidance how the need was to be met, and in what way He would save those otherwise certain to die. A serpent of bronze was to be made and set up on a pole. Those bitten had only to look at it to enjoy healing. Again, they acted in faith, and through such obedience found deliverance. 'So Moses made a bronze snake and put it up on a pole. Then when anyone was bitten by a snake and looked at the bronze snake, he lived.'

Not only so, we find in John 3:14,15 that Jesus Himself used this incident as an illustration of the purpose of the crucifixion in relation to the need of endangered sinners. He was similarly to be 'lifted up', that everyone might look to Him and be saved. So He said: 'Just as Moses lifted up the snake in the desert, so the Son of Man must be lifted up, that everyone who believes in him may have eternal life.' Salvation, therefore, is found, according to the gospel of Christ, through the acknowledgment of our need and dire peril because of sin, and through the obedience of faith in looking wholly to Christ crucified as the one necessary provision from God to secure deliverance and to make eternal life ours.

d) 2 Kings 5:1–14

Naaman, the Syrian, was a leper. He was led to look for healing from the God of Israel and His prophet Elisha. He had to learn the place and the necessity of the obedience of faith.

> So Naaman went with his horses and chariots and stopped at the door of Elisha's house. Elisha sent a messenger to say to him, "Go, wash yourself seven times in the Jordan, and your flesh will be restored and you will be cleansed." But Naaman went away angry and said, "I thought that he would surely come out to me and stand and call on the name of the LORD his God, wave his hand over the spot and cure me of my leprosy. Are not Abana and Pharpar, the rivers of Damascus, better than any of the waters of Israel? Couldn't I wash in them and be cleansed?" So he turned and went off in a rage.

Naturally he was not attracted by the Godly way and method of healing. But only when he mentally accepted it and actively submitted to it, did he find the desired cleansing. 'So he went down and dipped himself in the Jordan seven times, as the man of God had told him, and his flesh was restored and became clean like that of a young boy.'

Similarly we find, in the fulness of God's time, when God sent forth His Son to save us, that many took offence at the message which was preached, because it offered salvation from sin through Christ crucified for sinners. Such a message seemed to the cultured Gentile mind ridiculous, and to the religious Jewish mind blasphemous. How could public execution as a criminal and open exposure to the curse of heaven provide salvation for the world? Yet, this is the divinely appointed way of salvation, and the divinely provided remedy for sin. 'God made him who had no sin to be sin for us, so that in him we might become the righteousness of God.' (2 Cor. 5:21). And God is pleased to use this message, 'the message of the cross', 'to save those who believe' (see 1 Cor. 1:18–25).

The only sufficient and indispensable condition for enjoying the benefit of the gospel of saving grace is, therefore, the obedience of faith, that is, believing God means what He says and acting accordingly with hope fixed only and completely on Him and His faithful works.

2. The dead hear His voice

The word offered to sinners in the gospel is fundamentally a word of cleansing and renewal, offering forgiveness and new life. This is a word which is humanly impossible of fulfilment. Such a word can effectively be spoken only by God, who can both forgive sin and bring something out of nothing in new creation. For He can raise the dead; and so He calls the things which are not as though they are. This is the God who spoke to the fatherless Abram, the man with a childless wife, who was already past the normal age for bearing children, and renamed him 'Abraham', saying, 'You will be the father of many nations'. And Abram believed God, and was henceforth called 'Abraham'. Like the justified, who are reckoned righteous because of their faith in God, so Abraham was reckoned to be what as yet he was not. Also, by the obedience of faith he possessed the actual fulfilment of God's Word. He became a father; indeed, in believing God in this way, he became the father of all who believe from every nation. (See Rom. 4:16–22.)

So the divine word of the gospel, which sinners are to believe and to obey in order to be saved, is not only a word which directs and commands – as when Naaman was sent to the River Jordan to wash and be clean. Its very utterance also implies and guarantees accompanying divine power to make its fulfilment possible. Those who respond to it are in the first place not those who do anything to deserve salvation, but those to whom something transforming or regenerating is done – for only if this is true can they fulfil the activity of faith's obedience. Let's turn to the Bible for some illustrations.

a) Matthew 12:10a,13

'A man with a shrivelled hand was there.' A man who had clearly lost all power of using one of his hands is introduced to us. The one thing he could not do was to move it like the other hand. Yet this very thing which he could not do was the thing which the Saviour and the great Healer told him to do. 'Then he said to the man, "Stretch out your hand."' And in the obedience of faith the man did the humanly and naturally impossible. 'So he stretched it out and it was completely restored, just as sound as the other.' Similarly, when those powerless to serve God's will hear the Word of God in the gospel, in the obedience of faith they begin to do that which, without the re-creative power of God, would be utterly impossible. The outworked enjoyment of the inward benefit becomes theirs in the activity of faith's obedience. From then on their testimony is, 'He spoke, and it came to be' (Ps. 33:9).

b) Mark 2:1–12

In the incident of the healing of the helpless paralytic, who was carried to Jesus by four other men, and let down through the roof of a house to the feet of Jesus, an event of the same kind happened again. The man was told by Jesus to do the one thing he could not do – to get up, and take up his bed, and walk home. His immediate performance of this humanly impossible action was clearly made by Christ into a sign and proof of the man's release from the guilt and power of sin, and, more particularly, of the Saviour's own authority to give such release. Because of His power as the Son of man over areas completely outside an ordinary person's control, He was, and is, able to speak the kind of enabling Word, which opens up before the one who responds to it a new experience of both purifying and enlivening, of remission, and regeneration. So, as in the case of the helpless and sinful paralytic, response to this Word and its Author in the obedience of faith both brings the sinner into the enjoyment of peace with God, and brings the powerless into the experience of power to walk in God's way.

c) Mark 5:35–43; Luke 7:11–17; John 11:38–46

Outstanding illustrations of this truth that in the preaching of the gospel the dead hear God's voice were provided by Jesus on the three occasions when He restored to life the physically dead. On each occasion He addressed the dead body, and commanded the dead person to get up or come out; and on each occasion he or she acted accordingly. Living reappearance and return to ordinary human living immediately followed. Here clearly the Saviour spoke as one able to reach and to quicken into responsive action those who otherwise were beyond the reach of human calling, and were themselves unable to come back into life in the body. So, the word to which these dead responded was a word which carried with it the prevailing authority and the power adequate for its actual fulfilment. Those who heard it obviously believed it and the One who said it, and they visibly obeyed both it and Him.

Such illustrations help to confirm our understanding of the truth that the obedience of faith, which God commands in the gospel, is not only an obedience which He desires should be offered, but also an obedience which He makes possible. Consequently, the obedience of saving faith is more than the way of our response to enjoy the blessings of the gospel; it is rather the new way of our response to God, which is made possible by the gospel, or rather by God in the gospel. For He provides the grace or new life for its performance. We, therefore, who obey this word of saving grace come to know that such faith is no work or merit of theirs, but something possible only by the gift of God. In other words, this means that to set ourselves to live the life of faith's obedience to God's Word is but to seek to work out that salvation, which is first done deliberately for us and within us by God Himself. (See Phil. 2:12,13.)

The Word of God which comes to us sinners through the gospel is, therefore, like the voice of someone saying to a blind man in the dark, 'Read this', and simultaneously making reading possible by giving him both sight and light. It is like someone throwing wide a prison door as he says to the one confined within, 'Come out.' It is, as we have seen, like someone confronting a corpse, and saying to the departed dead person, 'Get up'; and he does so. Indeed, only a word from God which is in this way accompanied by His gift of light and freedom and life can offer an effective way of present salvation to those who are blind and caught in sin. It is to such a word and to such a God that sinners are invited, or rather commanded, in the gospel to render the obedience of faith.

Jesus said: 'I tell you the truth, whoever hears my word and believes him who sent me has eternal life and will not be condemned; he has crossed over from death to life. I tell you the truth, a time is coming and has now come when the dead will hear the voice of the Son of God and those who hear will live.' (John 5:24,25.) 'This is why it is said: "Wake up, O sleeper, rise from the dead, and Christ will shine on you."' (Eph. 5:14.)

5

True Discipleship

1. The significance of John 8:31,32

The principle of the obedience of faith in God and in His Word is not only the principle of entering into life; it is also the principle of enjoying life and finding its true fulfilment. In other words, it is the principle not just of gaining salvation from sin, but also of all subsequent true discipleship of Christ.

When the Saviour called men to follow Him and to become His disciples, the characteristic which He expected most was implicit response to His word in faith and obedience. So He broke into men's lives with the one absolute demand, 'follow me' – and He was satisfied, and appropriately answered, only when men left all and followed Him. To such followers He made it unmistakably plain that He expected unquestioning acceptance of His teaching and wholehearted action in obedience to it. He declared to such men that they would show their real attitude to Him by such obedience to His Word. He explicitly commanded that all who were subsequently made disciples should be taught to observe all things which He had commanded. (See Matt. 28:19,20.)

Let us consider His own statement of the condition of true discipleship: 'To the Jews who had believed him, Jesus said, "If you hold to my teaching, you are really my disciples. Then you will know the truth, and the truth will set you free."' (John 8:31,32).

It is instructive to notice when and to whom Jesus stated this condition of discipleship. It was to Jews who had reached the point of believing Him. The significance of this is that it indicates that, for those who would acknowledge Christ with a willingness to learn from Him, there is a point at the very beginning at which He demands that unquestioning loyalty should take the place of criticism. Critical inquiry and honest investigation are right and commendable as a means to discover the truth about Jesus. But once I know who He is, once I have reached the place where evidence demands that I recognize Him as trustworthy, then He asks nothing less than uncompromising and unconditional loyalty.

Indeed, no other method is possible. He cannot accept disciples who want themselves to choose the course and method of instruction. In His school these things are already fixed and cannot be altered to suit our whims or preferences. He cannot accept followers who want themselves to choose the path and set the lead. That was the nature of the issue when He spoke as He did to the Jews. Many Jews expected the Messiah, but they had their own ideas of what He ought to do. What some really hoped to do was to make the Messiah their servant, and to use His supernatural power to achieve their own ends. But such ideas the Christ Himself could not fulfil. (See, for example, John 6:15.) He had His own unalterable God-given plans. Those who would follow Him must accept His word as their law, otherwise unity of action would be impossible.

This issue is still a vital one for all who would be true disciples of Christ. For His ways are not our ways; and we cannot be true disciples unless we learn to give up our own ideas and to accept His. Consequently, as soon as people recognized who He was, and confessed their belief in Him, He confronted them with this necessary condition of progress in discipleship – 'hold to my teaching'. He cannot ask the world at large to accept His word in this way and to act on it, because some do not believe in Him; but He does make this demand of those who know who He is.

What if we live within His word like this? He promises that we shall know the truth, and that the truth will make us free. It is as we hold to, and act on, the truth which we do know that we discover or discern more of the truth. Therefore we are delivered from our own prejudices and misconceptions which would otherwise mislead us or hold us as slaves. Also we secure for ourselves the guarantee of continuance in our doing. For the Word of God endures for ever. (See 1 Pet. 1:23.) And if we make room for it to endure in us, if we ourselves, no matter how much we are pushed or enticed to depart from it, if we ourselves live in it, we shall remain and so will our actions, when others perish. For the one who lives and endures in the Word of God and so becomes the one who does the will of God is one who lives and endures for ever. (See 1 John 2:17.)

2. The example of Simon Peter

The faithful record in the gospel story of Peter's denial of the Lord is surely meant to make us pointedly aware that personal discipleship of Christ may begin right, last a long time, achieve much, and yet go fundamentally wrong, and need radical re-orientation and renewal. Let us see then what we can learn from this story concerning the condition of true discipleship.

a) Luke 5:1–11

As a disciple, Simon Peter began rightly. Luke's account here shows us this in out-worked practice. Here in the world of fishing, where he might have claimed to know all there was to know, and where a whole night's failure to catch fish suggested to natural judgment that it was foolish to try now, Simon immediately accepted the imperative word of Jesus as decisive. 'Master,' he answered – and let us note the word – 'Master, we've worked hard all night and haven't caught anything. But because you say so, I will let down the nets.' Nor was he then misled and disappointed. For 'when they had done so, they caught such a large number of fish that their nets began to break'. So Simon Peter exhibited in action his obedient faith in the Master's word, and its satisfying reward.

b) Matthew 16:15,16,21–23

Yet this exemplary disciple, so ready, when challenged, to confess his personal acknowledgement of Jesus as the Christ of God, went surprisingly wrong when the Saviour began the second stage of His teaching. For, once His Person was fully recognized by the chosen band of disciples, the Master went on to a second subject.

'From that time on Jesus began to explain to his disciples that he must go to Jerusalem and suffer many things at the hands of the elders, chief priests and teachers of the law, and that he must be killed and on the third day be raised to life.' Peter met this announcement not with the submissive acceptance of a true disciple but with the assertive and presumptuous rejection of a self-confident critic. 'Peter took him aside and began to rebuke him. "Never, Lord!" he said. "This shall never happen to you!"'

Such a complete change of attitude towards the Master happened when and where one would least expect it. It appeared in the leading disciple, shortly after he had made a personal and divinely inspired confession of who Christ is. Also, its sinful and evil character was little suspected, because in intention it was so well-meaning. For Peter's protest was, as he saw it, made on the highest religious grounds. Was it not his religious duty to protest? Did not the Scriptures foretell glory and sovereignty for God's Christ? Surely it was a shameful contradiction of His true destiny for Him to be put to death!

So Peter became involved, without realizing it (as quite a few still do today), in a fatal contradiction of attitude. He still called Jesus 'Lord'; and yet he openly opposed His Word and rejected His way. Nor did Jesus hide from Peter the gravity of such a change of attitude. He immediately and bluntly rebuked Peter for becoming an agent and mouthpiece of the devil, and a stumbling block in the way of the Master's progress; and all because he preferred his own human ideas to divine ones.

c) *Matthew 26:69–75*

Peter did not listen to the warning. He failed to comprehend not only its gravity, but even its truth. He went on blindly with a divided mind. He still was sure that Jesus was the Christ. But he would not have a Christ who must go to the cross. It was surely this divided mind that ultimately involved him in disowning his discipleship of Jesus as the Christ. For the unwanted suffering, so explicitly and repeatedly predicted, inevitably drew near. Jesus was arrested, mocked, ill-treated. Peter was asked whether he were not one of those who had followed Jesus as the Christ. 'A servant girl came to him. "You also were with Jesus of Galilee," she said. But he denied it before them all. "I don't know what you're talking about," he said.' And all because he had earlier and repeatedly refused to take to heart the God-given Word which was intended to prepare his mind to accept what he naturally did not want, but what God had eternally planned.

d) John 13:3–9

The Master, however, knew that, deep down, Peter's heart intention was right. He coveted glory and honour, not suffering and shame, for God's Christ. He had to learn that the shame was necessary first, and necessary as the price of his own salvation. So the loving Lord, who saw the inevitable denial that was impending, did not disown him as a disciple, and treat him as an unbeliever. Rather He prayed for him that his faith should not fail. (See Luke 22:31,32.) Also, He brought the fundamental issue home to Peter in the object lesson of the feet-washing. For when Jesus took a towel and a basin and began to wash His disciples' feet, Peter once more objected, and fundamentally for the same reason that he objected to the coming Cross, because be wanted to save his Master from humiliation. But, said Jesus in effect, the thing which you do not want, and cannot now understand, is the thing which is necessary for your benefit. Without it you cannot share in the kingdom of God.

'Unless I wash you, you have no part with me.' Faced with this ultimatum Peter returned to the proper attitude of discipleship, and accepted what as yet he did not understand, because the Lord said that it must be.

Nor is this story without its continuing application to many present-day disciples. There are still those who begin correctly in the simplicity of the unquestioning obedience of faith. But later, in the realm of the intellectual understanding of God's Word and God's ways, and the recognition of the necessity of Christ's substitutionary and penal death for the salvation of sinners, they are beset by difficulties, and even make their outspoken objections. Often, when their mind is thus wrongly divided, their heart is at bottom, like Peter's, still right. For such, return to harmony of mind and heart through understanding of God's way, and enjoyment of its saving benefit, can come, as it came to Peter, only through fresh submission to the God-given Word. This is for them, as for us all, the constant condition of true discipleship.

6

Perils in the Way

It is plain from the Old Testament and the New Testament alike that what God desires in His people is that they should be doers of the word and not hearers only. (See Jas 1:22,25.) It was in such terms that Moses charged Israel before his own death, and before they entered the promised land. So we read: 'Hear now, O Israel, the decrees and laws I am about to teach you. Follow them so that you may live and may go in and take possession of the land that the LORD, the God of your fathers, is giving you.' (Deut. 4:1; cf. 5:1; 6:1; 8:1; 11:1,32; 12:1).

In exhorting them to do the truth of God in this way, Moses also exhorted them to take particular care to do the whole truth, and to do nothing but the truth. In other words, he warned them both against including what God had not ordained, and against omitting what God had commanded. Only like this could they properly and fully keep His commandments. So we read: 'Do not add to what I command you and do not subtract from it, but keep the commands of the LORD your God that I give you'; and again later we read, 'See that you do all I command you; do not add to it or take away from it' (Deut. 4:2; 12:32). Similarly the closing words of Revelation, with which the New Testament ends, threaten the eternal judgment of God upon anyone who shall add to, or take away from, the words of this book. (See Rev. 22:18,19.) These, therefore, are persistent dangers. Let us consider them each in turn.

1. Adding to the Word of God

The danger of adding to the Word of God is a danger which besets people who are active in works of religious devotion. It is a subtle peril which besets the religiously minded, and often overtakes them unawares. This danger belongs to the ritualistic and the superstitious. It is the danger of the legalistic and conscientious, who put themselves under obligation to perform certain practices or to keep certain rules which are not from God, and whose performance does not please God or truly help others. Let's examine and really hear the rebuke of some biblical examples.

a) Isaiah 29:13

This tendency to add something not of divine appointment but of human devising may find expression in the professed worship of God Himself. So Isaiah was given a word from God to utter about the worship of the people of his day. 'The Lord says . . . Their worship of me is made up only of rules taught by men.' In other words, the forms they used to express professed reverence for God came from themselves and were not God-ordained; and their virtual condemnation here by the prophet implies that they involved practices displeasing to God.

b) Deuteronomy 4:9–12,15,16,23,24

Moses indeed gave a specific warning against this very danger in the charge whose opening words we have already quoted. He reminded them that the special revelation from God, which was granted to them at Sinai, was meant to teach them how to worship Him, and how to bring up their children to do the same. What they needed to remember was that in this revelation of God they 'heard the sound of words but saw no form; there was only a voice'. God made Himself known not in visible form but in intelligible utterance. Therefore in the congregation of His people, gathered to worship Him, they should beware of the natural desire to have some visible object or image towards which reverence can be physically directed. It is rather by prophetic utterance, by the preaching of the Word, that God is pleased to make men aware of His presence in their midst, and to call forth the worship of their adoration and believing response. So Paul wrote concerning the meeting of a Christian congregation

> But if an unbeliever or someone who does not understand comes in while everybody is prophesying, he will be convinced by all that he is a sinner and will be judged by all, and the secrets of his heart will be laid bare. So he will fall down and worship God, exclaiming, "God is really among you!" (1 Cor, 14:24,25).

We need to be careful, therefore, that in our Christian congregations, out of a natural desire to help worship, we wrongly add what God has not ordained. For the 'idol' that is given the worship that rightly belongs to God alone is offensive to him. Such worship, Moses said, 'the LORD your God has forbidden'. Nor let Israel forget that 'the LORD your God is a consuming fire, a jealous God'.

c) Matthew 15:1–9

Jesus condemned some of the religious practices of His day for the same reason, and in the strongest terms. When asked by the scribes and Pharisees why His disciples broke certain recognized religious observances, He charged them with introducing their own precepts to the exclusion of those of God. 'And why do you break the command of God for the sake of your tradition?' He said. So He called them 'hypocrites' or play-actors, acting a part which was not an expression of their real selves; and He endorsed the words of Isaiah as applying to them that 'These people honour me with their lips, but their hearts are far from me. They worship me in vain; their teachings are but rules taught by men.'

Thus the Saviour Himself taught that in the practice of religion artificial additions can completely invalidate the revealed truth of God and make His Word virtually inoperative. Nor did this corruption occur in the midst of unbelieving darkness but in the place of special religious privilege, in the place of revelation and God-given enlightenment, and among those professedly learned in the law of God and responsible to teach others of His ways.

2. Taking away from the Word of God

The opposite danger is the danger of diminishing or taking away, the danger of failing to accept and to respond to the whole Word of God. This had overtaken the Sadducees at that time, who said that there was 'no resurrection . . . neither angels nor spirits' (Acts 23:8). This is a danger which besets people who are intellectually active and are influenced by some prevailing philosophy or some current school of thought. It is the danger of the rationalist, the liberal, the modernist, who is unwilling to be bound by 'the faith that was once for all entrusted to the saints' (Jude 3). It is the danger of the student, who in the name of honest scientific investigation and inquiry for truth is persuaded to indulge in what is often presumptuous theorizing. Again, let's pay close attention to the warning of specific scriptural examples.

a) 1 Timothy 6:20,21

Here Timothy is told plainly and urgently that if he is to preserve faithfully the deposit of revealed truth, the very Word of God with which he has been entrusted, he must deliberately turn away from the godless nonsense and the speculative propositions and counter-arguments of those who in the name of so-called 'science' are opposing and abandoning the revealed truth of God. Timothy needs, it is implied, to beware of being fascinated and captivated by their pretensions to originality or thoroughness. His very love of the truth of God should give him an instinctive distaste for, and an aversion from, the error which opposes it.

For in such a situation the only alternative to allowing one's devotion to God-given truth to govern one's reaction is for oneself to be captured by some opposing new school of thought. While some still profess their continued loyalty to the God-given Word, others may profess their loyalty to some prevailing scientific theory. For example, they may become 'dialectical materialists'. The result is that such a theory, once they agree to it, influences their whole outlook. Such people no longer see things as they used to do. They cease to be simple believers in the God-given Word. They no longer hold to, or are held by, plain scriptural doctrines. As far as the true faith of Christ is concerned, they err and go astray.

b) 2 Timothy 2:16–18

Here the same warning is repeated, with more particular reference to specific error, to individuals who propagate it, and to the harm it must do. Such empty theorizing only promotes a decrease of true reverence for God. It tends to create an unhelpful atmosphere for study and righteous appreciation; sacred things cease to be sacred. Not only so, the particular theory of the month becomes dominant; and so people pay reverence, not to God and His Word, but to human authorities and 'their teaching'. In contrast to God's Word which brings life and health or can be eaten as nourishing food, this 'word' is like a malignant gangrene, which eats its way into healthy organisms, and works death and destruction. An illustration of such influence is found in Hymenaeus and Philetus and their teaching. For on the strength of their scientific theorizing or philosophical presuppositions they had apparently denied the possibility of a future resurrection of the body, and had thus robbed some of a precious fundamental of true Christian faith. Such taking away from the God-given Word is dishonouring to God and harmful to his children.

c) Acts 20:30,32

Finally, we need to notice again that such dangers can arise within the church. It is believers that may themselves go wrong, and then lead others astray. So Paul warned the elders of the church in Ephesus: 'Even from your own number men will arise and distort the truth in order to draw away disciples after them.' Here there is warning of the same trap noted above. Such false teachers entice men and women to become, not true disciples of Christ, but followers of themselves, and propagators of their false teaching.

For their safety and true edification Paul commended the Ephesian elders 'to God, and to the word of his grace'. It is through unquestioning faith in this God and this Word, and through obedience to Him and to it, without adding or taking away anything, that we, too, may be protected from error and progress in the truth.

7

The Practice of Obedience (1)

Those who would set themselves to be obedient and faithful to God and His Word soon find that they are involved in an activity which makes exacting and unceasing demands, which embraces the whole of living, and continues until the end of life's journey. Indeed, in the Christian experience nothing falls outside its concern. It is, therefore, impossible here to engage on any exhaustive treatment of the subject of this chapter. All we shall attempt (in the next chapter also) is to consider some of the demands such obedience makes on those sustaining its performance.

1. Endurance

This activity of obedience is an indispensable expression of a living faith. Without it faith is a worthless profession. What is more, the full response of faith to the God-given Word involves not only immediate obedience but also persistence to the end. We are called not only to begin but also to complete the course, to 'run with perseverance the race marked out for us' (Heb. 12:1). Such continuing response to God's Word may be of two kinds. Sometimes

God's Word demands active obedience to its command
or constraint. At other times it requires passive submission to its plain statement of truth, prohibition or
restraint. But in both kinds of response alike full possession of the reward of obedience commonly involves
holding on, whether in action or submission, till God's
time for fulfilment comes. Such experience puts to the
proof the faith which inspires our obedience. Thus the
testing of our faith demands, and is meant to produce,
patience or continuance in well-doing; and only if such
patience, or endurance, is allowed to bring its work to
completion, can we ourselves reach the intended goal, or
possess the promised inheritance.

So we read: 'Consider it pure joy, my brothers, whenever you face trials of many kinds, because you know
that the testing of your faith develops perseverance.
Perseverance must finish its work so that you may be
mature and complete, not lacking anything' (Jas 1:2–4).
And again: 'We want each of you to show this same diligence to the very end, in order to make your hope sure.
We do not want you to become lazy, but to imitate those
who through faith and patience inherit what has been
promised' (Heb. 6:11,12).

The danger is that, in the midst of the pathway of
faith's obedience, we give up its pursuit and fail to reach
the intended goal. To Christians thus tempted to turn
aside in the middle, and to abandon the continuance of
faith's active expression in obedience, the writer of
Hebrews instructed: 'So do not throw away your confidence; it will be richly rewarded. You need to persevere
so that when you have done the will of God, you will
receive what he has promised' (Heb. 10:35,36). Let us
then consider in detail some biblical illustrations from
which we may learn these two things; first, the need for
the obedience which faith inspires to be sustained to the

end; and second, the inevitability of such faith being tested in order that its capacity for successful endurance may stand revealed.

a) Hebrews 11:30

'By faith the walls of Jericho fell, after the people had marched around them for seven days.' This brief statement refers to the familiar story of the capture of Jericho by the Israelites, a story recorded at length in Joshua 6: the significant fact was that the victory was God-given. He made the walls of Jericho to fall down flat. This conquest was possessed by the Israelites through the obedience of faith. But, unlike those bitten by snakes in the wilderness, who were immediately healed when they looked at the brazen serpent, they did not experience the victory at once. On this occasion faith had to sustain the activity of obedience to God's command for a full seven days. Only after this persistence of believing obedience was complete did the walls fall down. Thus it is plain that progress in possession of the promised land depended upon the endurance of faith's obedience. This illustrates the governing principle of all true progress in Christian discipleship. One needs not only a faith which obeys God's Word, but also a faith which keeps on obeying. One needs not only a faith which looks to God in hope, but also a faith which is content to wait in confident expectation until God's time for fulfilment comes. So God's prophet was inspired to utter words such as, 'the one who trusts will never be dismayed' and 'Blessed are all who wait for him!' (Isa. 28:16; 30:18).

b) Matthew 8:23–27

(See also Mark 4:35–41; Luke 8:22–25.) Trouble and danger quickly reveal the strength or weakness of one's professed confidence. Its capacity or inability to endure the strain of possible severe testing is then discovered; and by such experience faith itself is disciplined, developed and matured. In the incident recorded here there is an illustration of faith being tested and found wanting or incomplete. The disciples followed Jesus into a ship. They went on board, not by their own initiative or decision, but as disciples following their Master. It was, therefore, by His leading that they were on the sea. Consequently the Lord Himself was responsible for the safety and the issues of the crossing.

Indeed, He had assured them of the destination in view, when 'he gave orders to cross to the other side of the lake' Yet, when a huge storm suddenly overtook them, the disciples abandoned the faith of true discipleship in which they came on board. They lost their pro-per confidence. Panicking and afraid, they awoke the sleeping Jesus, and virtually accused Him of indifference. 'Master, carest thou not? we perish!' (KJV). The Master quickly asserted His sovereign command over the wind and the waves. He got up and stilled the storm and there was a great calm. The storm was no cause of alarm or fear to Him. But what did distress and disappoint Him was the failure of His disciples' faith. So, since He had them alone and away from onlookers who might overhear, He bluntly reprimanded them. 'You of little faith, why are you so afraid?' How often do we not deserve similar reprimand? Not in the spirit of unbelief and fear can God's Word be obeyed, its assurance enjoyed, and its promise possessed.

c) Acts 23:11; 27:20–25,44b

A similar story, but one recording a better response of faith on the part of the Christian, is to be found in Acts

27. For, while on the journey to Rome as a prisoner, Paul was involved in a prolonged storm of such severity that in the human judgment of those on board the ship 'finally gave up all hope of being saved'. Yet Paul did not lose hope. He held on to the God-given Word, and found in it assurance of deliverance. For, long before this journey began, while Paul was still in Jerusalem, the Lord had said to him, 'Do not be afraid, Paul. You must stand trial before Caesar; and God has graciously given you the lives of all who sail with you.' So Paul believed that, if he was to bear witness in Rome, he could not perish on the journey; he must be saved out of the storm. Now, on the storm-tossed ship, not only was this hope confirmed, but also the assurance was added that all his fellow-travellers would be saved, too. So Paul stood forth openly on the deck to cheer up his dejected and despairing fellow-travellers, by telling them of his faithful expectation. '*I exhort you,*' he said,

> Keep up your courage, because not one of you will be lost; only the ship will be destroyed. Last night an angel of the God whose I am and whom I serve stood beside me and said, 'Do not be afraid, Paul. You must stand trial before Caesar; and God has graciously given you the lives of all who sail with you.' So keep up your courage, men, for I have faith in God that it will happen just as he told me.

Nor was this vain imagination, the delusion of wishful thinking: 'In this way everyone reached land in safety.'

d) 2 Kings 4:8–37

The story of the Shunammite woman recorded here affords an even more outstanding illustration of holding on without wavering to an assurance previously given.

For, in fulfilment of the Word of the Lord, spoken to her by the prophet Elisha, this woman was given a son. After a few years the child died. What did the mother do? She did not bury the child; she went up and laid the dead body on the bed of the man of God. Why? She was throwing back responsibility to the place where it belonged. Her attitude was that, if God and His prophet had given her a child when natural hope of children was at an end, it was, so to speak, their responsibility and not hers to complete what they had begun, and to put right what had apparently gone fatally wrong in the middle. For, to such a woman, the promise of a son meant the continuation of the family through his descendants. So she held on to the faith of the beginnings of her mother-hood, the faith in which the child was born.

This attitude of holding on to the assurance that this thing was a divine undertaking, and not a mere human and personal responsibility, gave her peace and hope where otherwise there would have been none. Leaving the dead body on the prophet's bed, she set off at once to find the man of God himself to commit the matter to him. To others she would betray no anxiety, for the burden was not hers but his. Why then should she be anxious? She answered, 'Peace; all is well.' But as soon as she got to Elisha himself, she threw all the burden on him, and would not leave him to go back to the child without him. For the child was not hers by her desire but by the man of God's promise. Therefore, he must come to save; and he did. The woman took back her son alive from the hands of Elisha.

Hers is an example to be followed. Often hopes seem to fail, or even to come to an end, before they have reached maturity and fulfilment. The temptation then is to let go faith, to give up hope. This is how the Israelites failed on the wilderness road between Egypt and

Canaan. The success of winning through the trials of the journey between the birth of first beginnings and the full-grown adulthood of completed purpose comes only to those who, like the Shunammite woman, refuse to abandon God-given assurance. 'We have come to share in Christ if we hold firmly till the end the confidence we had at first.' (Heb. 3:14).

2. Unreserved confidence in God

No man will thus hold on in the pathway of faith's obedience, unless he has complete confidence in God's faithfulness. He must know whom He has believed, and be absolutely sure that He will keep His word. For God cannot deny Himself. As Balaam said long ago: 'God is not a man, that he should lie, nor a son of man, that he should change his mind. Does he speak and then not act? Does he promise and not fulfill?' (Num. 23:19). Similarly the God-inspired Word given to comfort the believing soul that is tired and despondent, because his road is temporarily dark, strikes the same emphasis. For in such circumstances the only satisfying activity is to rest on God and to count on His faithfulness. So we read: 'Who among you fears the LORD and obeys the word of his servant? Let him who walks in the dark, who has no light, trust in the name of the LORD and rely on his God.' (Isa. 50:10).

a) Rom. 4:17–21

Abraham, the man of faith, outstandingly exemplifies this spirit. He was sure that God would not promise anything unless He both could do it, and also actually intended to do it. So, in utterly hopeless natural circumstances, and through prolonged delay and human disappointment, he hopefully believed. Thus Isaac was born. 'And so after waiting patiently, Abraham received what was promised.' (Heb. 6:15).

b) Heb. 11:17–19

And this is not all. For God allowed Abraham to be further tested still. The man whose hopes of the fulfilment of God's promises concerning his seed were all invested in Isaac, heard the call to offer him up as a burntoffering. But how could he? How could he sacrifice Isaac, when it meant putting an end to all his hopes – hopes which were not of sight, but of faith, and not of men but of God? If God intended to make Isaac's posterity a great nation, how could He mean Abraham to put Isaac to death? To natural reckoning the two things were contradictory and irreconcilable. But, because he knew in whom he was believing, Abraham knew that, if he acted in obedience, and performed the deed which would put an end to all his hopes, then, because he had obeyed God, God must do something to make the impossible possible.

Consequently, under the pressure of such an apparently insoluble problem, the hope of resurrection was born. For, if the fulfilment of God's promises necessitated Isaac being alive, and yet obedience to God had demanded that Isaac must first die, then God must be going to bring him to life again. So did faith reckon; and so is undreamt of, supernatural hope born to faith when continuance in obedience to God and His Word brings natural hope to an end.

Such obedience is therefore the way of faith's full possession. And the secret of persevering in obedience, when obedience seems to shut us in, to darken our way, and even to threaten the loss of everything, is faith in the promises of God –and God is sure to fulfil His Word. 'The one who calls you is faithful and he will do it' (1 Thes. 5:24). For when we respond to the call of His Word, not only do we move in obedience, God also moves to fulfil His Word. The hope of safe emergence from the trial, the hope of successful possession of faith's reward, rests on God's doing not on ours. As we trust and obey, and risk all on Him, God carries us through. Nor is there any other way to reach the goal of His purpose and to enjoy the best blessings of His giving. Indeed, the very pressure of God's hand in the discipline of life's circumstances constrains us, by shutting us in, to find this way of faith's obedience as the only way out.

> But we never can prove
> The delights of His love,
> Until all on the altar we lay;
> For the favour He shows,
> And the joy He bestows,
> Are for them who will trust and obey.

3. A good conscience

Those who would thus prove God's faithfulness must expect to have their own faithfulness put to the proof by the God with whom they are brought into fellowship. For no one can fully enter into the satisfaction of taking God at His Word, and of enjoying the fulfilment of His promises, unless by God's grace he becomes the kind of person whose own word can be trusted and whose corresponding action can be counted on. In other words, the one who would truly obey God's Word must do so with absolute singleness and sincerity of heart; and this sincerity must be demonstrated in his or her actions as well as in his or her words by diligent wholehearted observance of God's commandments. This means, to quote the psalmist's language, that he must walk blamelessly (Ps. 84:11).

a) *Amos 5:14,15,21–24; Micah 6:6–8*

Here there is no room for compromise or hypocrisy. Outward profession and superficial practice of religious devotion, which are unsupported by serious heart intention and by corresponding upright behaviour are only hateful to God and unsatisfying to our neighbours; they deceive none but those absorbed in doing them. The Bible bears repeated witness to this. For instance, God spoke through Amos to the Israel of his day, and said: 'Seek good, not evil, that you may live.

Then the LORD God Almighty will be with you, just as you say he is. Hate evil, love good; maintain justice in the courts. Perhaps the LORD God Almighty will have mercy on the remnant of Joseph.'

And again,

> "I hate, I despise your religious feasts; I cannot stand your assemblies. Even though you bring me burnt offerings and grain offerings, I will not accept them. Though you bring choice fellowship offerings, I will have no regard for them. Away with the noise of your songs! I will not listen to the music of your harps. But let justice roll on like a river, righteousness like a never-failing stream.

Or similarly Micah prophesied:

> With what shall I come before the LORD and bow down before the exalted God? Shall I come before him with burnt

offerings, with calves a year old? Will the LORD be pleased with thousands of rams, with ten thousand rivers of oil? Shall I offer my firstborn for my transgression, the fruit of my body for the sin of my soul? He has showed you, O man, what is good. And what does the LORD require of you? To act justly and to love mercy and to walk humbly with your God.

b) 1 Timothy 1:3–7

The one who obeys God's Word must become someone whose life is wholly devoted to the expression of true love towards God and his or her neighbours. There can be no question that this truth is supported by the cumulative witness of both Old and New Testaments. But such love cannot be practised where heart sincerity is lacking. So Paul said, with reference to his solemn exhortation to Timothy, 'The goal of this command is love, which comes from a pure heart and a good conscience and a sincere faith.' Such a statement explicitly indicates that there are searching moral conditions of true spiritual devotion. Deep down within one must mean what one professes without pretence or superficiality. One must be careful and active conscientiously to live up to all the light which one has. One's motive must be single and sincere, undivided and undefiled.

What is equally plain is that the possession of such purity of heart and life, or the maintenance of its unceasing pursuit, depends upon the attitude and action of the individual believer. It is possible for us to abandon the maintenance of such standards. We may, for instance, turn aside to interests and activities which still have to do with the God-given Word, but which are not in the pathway of its true obedience. We may even satisfy our desires to become teachers in such matters, only to

become involved in things which are inevitably profit-
less. Indeed, Paul plainly indicates here that such interests issue only in unprofitable arguing about supposed
problems, and in the discussion of empty trivialities,
instead of in promoting the upbuilding of God's people
in the way of faith. Or, as H.P. Liddon put it, such stud-
ies 'do more to suggest points for controversy than to
illustrate the divine dispensation (of redemption), which
is only understood in the sphere of faith'. What this kind
of person needs to learn is that there is a right and a
wrong use to be made of the law of God, and that it
proves its excellence and brings benefit to the user only
when it is used properly.

c) 1 Timothy 1:18–20

Here (later in the same chapter) Paul repeats his insis-
tence on the necessity of preserving a good conscience,
as an indispensable prerequisite of continuing soundness in the faith. He names two individuals, the tragedy
of whose spiritual career provided concrete evidence
and warning of the fact that no one can disregard the
demands of conscience and still continue true to the
Christian faith. For these people, by their deliberate
indifference to moral standards – they 'rejected' or 'put
away' a good conscience – involved their course as
Christian believers in disaster; they 'so have ship-
wrecked their faith' (KJV). For no one can disregard the
witness of conscience and still hold to a safe course in
the truth: 'A true belief will not long survive unfaithful-
ness to God's inward voice' (H.P. Liddon).

Some years ago I had occasionally to travel by small
river boat in West China. Here there are often stretches of
rapid water, difficult and dangerous to navigate. A traveller has to entrust his life to the acquired knowledge and

skill of his Chinese boatmen. They surprised me at first, on going downstream in the rapids, by their energetic determination to make the boat go faster still. As rapid water is approached all available hands took to the oars and paddled hard, as if progress depended on their efforts; and in one very practical sense it did, and still does – and not only progress but also safety. If the many rocks and boulders are to be avoided in the swift moving water, and the boat saved from shipwreck, she must be effectively steered. However no boat will respond to her rudder unless she is moving in relation to the water in which she is to be steered. To yield to the fascinating delusion that the swift moving water is surely carrying them forward fast enough, without the need of additional effort on their part, would only involve the boatmen in certain disaster. For, at the crucial moment, the boat would not respond to the steersman. The very current that is carrying them forward would then only bring about their damage and possible destruction by dashing the boat on to the rocks.

So faith in the current is not sufficient; indeed, by itself it may be perilously misleading. There must be determined and energetic attention to the task and responsibility of steering to the right hand or to the left. Those who neglect this duty will not be carried forward to their desired destination. Similarly, those who know how much all true spiritual progress depends upon faith in the movement towards them in grace of the living God cannot afford to forget that, if they would continue to enjoy the benefits of God-given life and salvation, they must train their senses to discern between good and evil; and they must alertly and energetically hold fast to a good conscience.

It is helpful to remember here how Jesus answered the devil's second temptation. When invited to throw

Himself down from a pinnacle of the temple, and to trust in God and His promises of preservation, it was His conscience rather than His faith that replied that it would be wrong: 'It is also written: "Do not put the Lord your God to the test."' (Matt. 4:5–7).

d) Proverbs 16:6

'Through the fear of the LORD a man avoids evil.' According to the Old Testament Scriptures the first principle of life to be taught to children is active reverence for the living God. 'The fear of the LORD is the beginning of wisdom' (Ps. 111:10). In other words, proper reverence for God is the indispensable foundation of all right understanding. Only in God's light can we see. (See Ps. 36:9.) The same principle is expressed in the New Testament by statements such as 'physical training is of some value, but godliness has value for all things' (1 Tim. 4:8); 'We live by faith, not by sight' (2 Cor. 5:7);

'By faith we understand . . .' (Heb. 11:3). According to the same Old Testament Scriptures the next thing to be taught to the growing child is moral discernment. The child must learn in the fear of God 'to reject the wrong and choose the right' (Isa. 7:15,16). Similarly, the sign of Christian growth to maturity is 'by constant use' to have trained one's senses 'to distinguish good from evil' (Heb. 5:14). It is only by the combination of these two activities of reverence for God and moral discrimination that life can be rightly directed; for to avoid shipwreck one must hold both faith and a good conscience.

e) Psalms 119:11

'I have hidden your word in my heart that I might not sin against you.' Believers are clearly meant to grow in powers of moral discernment by their increasing knowledge of the Word of God, and their growing ability to apply it. The Bible abounds in plain instructions concerning personal behaviour; it indicates the principles which should govern conduct. In many matters in life the Bible leaves us in no doubt which way is right and which way is wrong. It is according to one's measure of knowledge that conscience can and ought to function to approve or disapprove, to constrain or restrain. 'Anyone, then, who knows the good he ought to do and doesn't do it, sins' (Jas 4:17). Such obligations governing behaviour operate in relation first to God, then to others, and finally to oneself. They embrace and concern every activity and relationship of human life. Only those can and do fully obey God's Word and enjoy its promised blessings, who make it their diligent and unceasing concern to be well-pleasing to the Lord in everything they do. So there is a need for each of us to live in a way that means we can say, as Paul said of himself 'So I strive always to keep my conscience clear before God and man' (Acts 24:16).

8

The Practice of Obedience (2)

The gospel of God's saving grace demands, as we have seen, our obedience to the life-giving Lord, if we are to enjoy the benefits and true salvation. Obedience to the truth of the gospel does not, however, end there. Those who enter into the sphere of its blessing find themselves by God's appointment inevitably involved in a twofold stewardship. It becomes their privilege and responsibility on the one hand to communicate it to others, and on the other hand to preserve whole and entire, the very Word of God's saving grace to which they owe their salvation, and their consequent membership in the people of God. We will now consider these two responsibilities.

1. Propagating the gospel

If, as true disciples of Christ, we are to become fully obedient to His Word, there is one plain demand of His whose challenge we must face, and that is the demand to make Him known as the Saviour of men. For the risen Lord explicitly commissioned His followers to proclaim to all the gospel. So we cannot be fully obedient to His

Word unless we take our share in the discharge of this commission.

a) Matthew 28:19,20; Mark 16:15; Luke 24:44–48; John 20:21–23

Each one of the four accounts includes as it closes explicit mention of this missionary commission. So we read in Matthew 28:19,20: 'Therefore go and make disciples of all nations, baptizing them in the name of the Father and of the Son and of the Holy Spirit, and teaching them to obey everything I have commanded you.' Likewise in Mark 16:15: 'Go into all the world and preach the good news to all creation.'

In Luke 24:44–48 there is a significant explanatory statement. We are told that the risen Lord showed clearly to His disciples from the Scriptures that His suffering and His resurrection were both fulfilments of what the Scriptures foretold, and that they accomplished God's planned purpose. It was therefore necessary that He should so suffer and rise again. Now, He asserted, because this necessary work has been accomplished, there is, as the prophecies of the Old Testament had foreshadowed, a gospel to be preached – a gospel of salvation from sin, the benefits of which can be freely offered to the whole world. Now, He said, God intends 'repentance and forgiveness of sins will be preached in his name to all nations'. Also, He said, that the place to begin the preaching is 'at Jerusalem'; in other words, the gospel is to be preached to the Jews first, and then to the Gentiles. He added, 'You are witnesses of these things'; or, as we might say, 'you are the people to do the preaching.'

In effect Jesus said: I have done the indispensable work of redemption and reconciliation. You are to do the

complementary work of declaration and encouragement, offering others salvation through Christ's finished
work, and beseeching them to make their peace with
God. Here then we have the divine authority, the scriptural sanction, and the Master's own charter for world-
wide Christian missionary effort, and for our place in it
as Christ's witnesses. For it is God's eternal purpose
thus to provide salvation in Christ; to this the Old
Testament bears witness. This purpose has been fulfilled; Christ has died for our sins, and He is risen and
all-powerful to save; so present salvation is available.
But we all will enjoy this benefit, only if news of it is
communicated. This communication is a task committed
by Christ to His followers. Those who become believers
in Christ and disciples of Christ are then meant by God's
appointment and Christ's command to take some share
in winning others to become His disciples.

The words recorded in John 20:21–23 indicate, if possible still more profoundly, the direct sanction from God
and the serious and eternal character of such service. For
Christ's commission to His disciples to preach salvation
to the world is similar and complementary to His own
commission as the Son of God to be the Saviour of the
world. This Christ made plain when He said, 'As the
Father has sent me, I am sending you'. Not only so: He
went on to indicate that those who engage in this ministry are to be empowered for it by the God-given Spirit,
and will thus share in a task which settles for ever the
eternal destiny of the human race. For, if the preacher of
this gospel offers sinners salvation in Christ's name, and
the sinners believe in the Saviour, then those sinners find
eternal forgiveness. Their sins will never again be
charged against them. So, said the Master to the commissioned preachers, 'If you forgive anyone his sins,
they are forgiven'. In other words, to lead others in

repentance and faith to obey the gospel and to trust in the Saviour is to do work of eternal moment, whose results will live for ever. Similarly, and even more solemnly, when any hear the gospel from human preachers and reject it, they are risking eternal condemnation. Their sins remain with them, and there irremovably remain. So, said the Master to His commissioned preachers, 'if you do not forgive them, they are not forgiven'. What is more, Christ spoke not to the eleven only but to a general gathering of disciples. These words, therefore, are not words authorizing a formal priestly absolution to be given only by some select and privileged hierarchy. They are rather words indicating the permanent character of the commission to evangelize, which rests upon all Christ's followers.

b) Matthew 14:15–21; 15:21–28,32–38

Now that we know what was the ultimate view it is helpful to look earlier and see how these ideas were anticipated in Jesus' teaching of the disciples. By some of the things which He did with them, or allowed them to do with Him, during His earthly ministry, Jesus was preparing their minds, in ways which they did not appreciate at the time, for the full task of the future. Let us consider, for instance, the familiar stories of the feeding of the thousands. Here on two different occasions we find Christ working a miracle to provide supplies, and then using the disciples to get the supplies distributed. He was the indispensable Master workman; yet He deliberately made them into necessary fellow-workers. The one source from which the supplies all came was Himself. The loaves became more than enough for all when He broke them. But although His hand alone could break the bread, it was His chosen method that the broken pieces should reach the needy not by His hand but by the hands of the disciples. So 'he gave . . . to the disciples, and the disciples gave them to the people'. Thus in the simplest form is illustrated the staggering truth that once we know Him and become His followers, we stand between His saving grace and a needy world, as those who are entrusted with the privilege and responsibility of carrying to others the knowledge of the saving grace of Christ. So, when we would 'send the crowds away', He says, 'They do not need to go away. You give them something to eat.'

Also, while the first feeding was of a Jewish crowd, there is evidence for supposing that the second feeding was of a Gentile one. For it is written about them, as though they were not Israelites, that 'they praised the God of Israel' (Matt. 15:31). And between the two stories comes the story of the Syro-Phoenician woman, who was a Gentile. She came begging Christ to have mercy on her. Before He met her need, He asked, 'Is it right to take the children's bread, and to cast it to dogs?' (KJV). In other words, it was as if He were asking, 'If God provides bread for His children, to whom should it be given? To Jews only? Or also to people of other nations?' Then He answered both the request of the woman and His own question by ministering to her need, not because she was a Jew, but because she was a believer. He said to her,

'Woman, you have great faith! Your request is granted.' In this way He 'gave bread' to a Gentile believer. Similarly, shortly afterwards He gave actual bread to the Gentile multitude. Surely He was thus teaching His disciples that the salvation which He had come into the world to provide was for the Jews of course, but also for the world; indeed, in the second feeding He actually used them in ministry to feed Gentiles. So were their minds prepared to appreciate later that the gospel was to be preached 'first for the Jew, then for the Gentile' (Rom. 1:16), and that it was their business and responsibility to preach it. This is still the responsibility of all true disciples of Christ, to see that the spiritually hungry are given the Bread of Life.

c) 2 Corinthians 5:18–20

If we turn to the epistles we find the same ideas endorsed by the witness of the apostles. In particular notice how the apostle Paul was made to share in the same awareness and the same convictions. In 2 Corinthians 5:18–20 he declares that God has done two complementary things. He has 'reconciled us to himself through Christ'; and He has 'gave us the ministry of reconciliation'. He entrusted to Christ the work of reconciliation, He has 'committed to us the message of reconciliation'. On the cross Christ took our place as sinners and bore sin's condemnation. Now we are to take His place in the mission field of the world, and to encourage our neighbours to accept God's terms of peace, and to be reconciled to God. Such gospel witness, such missionary work, is nothing less than a complementary part of God's purpose for the redemption of all and our reconciliation to Him, complementary that is to the work of Christ's own death for our sins. These two activities belong together, the finished work of Christ on the cross and the continued witness in the world of His ambassadors. Just as Christ had of divine necessity to suffer and to rise again, so must 'this gospel . . . be preached in the whole world as a testimony to all nations', only 'then the end will come' (Matt. 24:14; Mark 13:10). There is, therefore, no more glorious task, no higher vocation, no better obedience, than to publish to needy sinners heaven's good news of salvation and so to become a fellow-worker with God and a partner in Christ's business, the Christ who said – and still says – 'Follow me and I will make you fishers of men' (Matt. 4:19).

2. Preserving the witness

If the truth of the gospel is to be faithfully preached and propagated in the world in this way, it must first of all be carefully preserved without addition or diminution by those who hold it in trust; and also faithfully handed on intact both to new adherents to the faith, and to the rising generation. Only so will the regions beyond and the children yet unborn receive in its fulness the God-given truths without loss or perversion.

a) 1 Timothy 6:20; 2 Timothy 2:2

In the New Testament epistles workers for God are solemnly charged first to guard the deposit of truth – to keep that which is committed to their trust – and then carefully to hand it on to others, who in their turn will do the same. So Paul wrote to Timothy 'guard what has been entrusted to your care', and later, 'And the things you have heard me say in the presence of many witnesses entrust to reliable men who will also be qualified to teach others.'

The ideas underlying these exhortations are covered in Article 20 of The 39 Articles of the Church of England by the statement that the Church of England is 'a witness and a keeper of holy Writ'. The emphasis here on the written form of God's Word is important. For the expression of the gospel and of the teaching of our Lord, which we have in the apostolic writings of the New

Testament, has given them a permanent fixed form of known limits, sometimes called the canon of Scripture. And it is the calling and the responsibility of God's people to preserve and to proclaim the witness of this inspired Word of God by guarding it in its entirety, as something God-given for our learning, and by testifying to its authority by using it as the determinative rule of faith and practice and the decisive textbook of all preaching and teaching.

b) Galatians 2:1–16

All Christians share to some extent in this stewardship of the God-given Word and in the responsibility to maintain unimpaired the apostolic succession of witness to the truth. This responsibility obviously rests particularly and most directly on those called of God to the public ministry of His Word in preaching and teaching. So Paul wrote of himself and of others like him such as Apollos or Peter: 'So then, men ought to regard us as servants of Christ and as those entrusted with the secret things of God. Now it is required that those who have been given a trust must prove faithful.' (1 Cor. 4:1,2).

This faithful preservation of the witness ought to be maintained, not just in defensive self-preservation, but rather in a spirit of positive self-sacrificing devotion to the continuance of the witness and work of the gospel of God in the world. In other words, it ought to be done, and it needs to be done, in the interest of the salvation of the lost; in the interest, that is, of giving to all and preserving for the future – for the world, for our children, and indeed for ourselves – the full and true gospel of salvation.

What the discharge of this responsibility may involve, and why such action may be necessary, are shown very clearly in Galatians. Here we find genuine converts to faith in Christ and the gospel of saving grace being perverted through being taught things radically different. Here we find Paul, back from the mission field, in the home church of Jerusalem itself, having to resist pressure (to have Titus circumcised) that he saw would deprive converts in the churches of Galatia of their liberty in Christ and bring them under the bondage of legalism (and ceremonialism). Here we find Paul at Antioch having publicly to withstand even Peter to the face, because, in changing his behaviour as a Christian, Peter ceased to walk uprightly according to the truth of the gospel. Paul did this because he saw clearly what was at stake; 'that the truth of the gospel', as he puts it, 'might continue with you' (KJV) (i.e., you Galatians or mission-field converts). He stood firm and made his protest because he saw that to yield on such a point would be to betray Christian liberty, gospel truth and Gentile evangelism. How important it is, therefore, that today, as we continue to support and send out missionaries, we should still recognize that, if full loyalty to the truth of the gospel is not preserved in the home churches by unyielding constancy and by possible necessary protest even in high places, the same truth of the gospel will soon no longer be preached and practised in its full purity and entirety in the churches of the mission field. There is still need, therefore, for faithful stewards of the God-given Word to 'contend for the faith that was once for all entrusted to the saints' (Jude 3), and to oppose the subtle or specious introduction of doctrines and practices, which involve nothing less than a return to legalism, a denial of salvation only by grace and through faith, and a departure from the pathway of true loyalty to the very gospel of God.

c) 2 Timothy 1:12–14

In this connection it is important to remember that, because soundness in the faith is not a matter merely of theoretical correctness of ideas but rather concerns one's vital spiritual well-being in the life of true discipleship, there are inevitable moral conditions of continuing in spiritual health. This is a truth of which we have already taken notice when considering the need to preserve a good conscience. The same truth is enforced here by Paul's words to Timothy. Those who would 'keep as the pattern of sound teaching' must do so 'with faith and love in Christ Jesus'. For unless true Christian faith and love are vitally active in one's life one cannot properly share in preserving the witness for the truth of the gospel.

Finally, in this task of preserving the witness, we can always count upon the unfailing help of God Himself. A possible rendering of the Greek of 2 Timothy 1:12 justifies the translation in the NRSV: 'for I know the one in whom I have put my trust, and I am sure that he is able to guard until that day what I have entrusted to him'. In this same context Paul also reminds Timothy that the Holy Spirit is given to dwell in the people of God for this very purpose – to preserve the witness (cf. Acts 1:8). God Himself can therefore be counted on to guard His own truth. He will not leave Himself without witness. And as those to whom He has given His Spirit we are called to be fellow-workers with God and with one another in this task of 'contending as one man for the faith of the gospel' (Phil. 1:27).

9

The Ultimate Issues

Obeying God's Word is of supreme importance because of its certain consequences or crowning rewards. God's Word is never an end in itself. It always has an end in view. God's speaking is always complemented by His doing. So we read: 'For he spoke, and it came to be; he commanded, and it stood firm.' (Ps. 33:9); and 'Does he speak and then not act? Does he promise and not fulfill?' (Num. 23:19). Similarly one's reaction and response to the Word of God, whether in obedience or disobedience, must inevitably issue in some corresponding fulfilment, some evident result. It is a distinctive characteristic of the inspired Word of God to make unmistakably plain what these ultimate issues are, and to challenge us to let our present activity be determined completely in the light of them. It is equally characteristic of the inspired Word of God that it distinguishes clearly two, and only two, alternatives, the pathway of obedience and the pathway of disobedience, leading to their inevitable and completely different ends, ends as different in essential character as light and darkness, life and death. We will, therefore, consider in this last chapter these alternatives and their ultimate issues.

1. The alternatives

The only alternative to obedience is disobedience. But those who fall into it are rarely aware of the true character and gravity of their action. For it begins in a less assertive form as simply a failure to do what God has commanded; and the very person who does this may be blinded to the seriousness of such failure by the satisfaction he finds in having heard God's Word, and in apparently knowing all about it. He is therefore able to make a profession of discipleship, and to answer all the questions; but he is not a doer.

a) Matthew 7:21–27

At the end of the Sermon on the Mount, after Jesus had given the disciples much teaching, He spoke abruptly and graphically warning of the folly of the failure to listen. This failure, when the real test comes, must end in inevitable disaster. These words with which Jesus finished His teaching are, in a very significant sense, the last words on this subject. It is well worth noting them. 'Not everyone who says to me, "Lord, Lord," will enter the kingdom of heaven, but only he who does the will of my Father who is in heaven . . . But everyone who hears these words of mine and does not put them into practice is like a foolish man who built his house on sand. The rain came down, the streams rose, and the winds blew and beat against that house, and it fell with a great crash.'

b) John 8:31–34

The Saviour made practical adherence to His teaching and sustained observance of His commands an indispensable condition of true discipleship, the condition both of knowing the truth and of finding in its knowledge true freedom. He went on to state with equal clarity and dogmatic brevity the only alternative. To human reckoning there may seem many roads to choose between, other than the one narrow road of devotion to the Master's Word. But Christ embraced all such possible roads under the one description of sinning or missing the mark. For they all involve failure to do the right, and the inevitable consequence of failure to reach the true goal of human existence – the glorious liberty of the children of God. Not only so, they all involve not only the ultimate consequence, but also the immediate result here and now, of bondage. For, as Jesus emphatically said, 'everyone who sins is a slave to sin'. So the only alternative to God-given freedom is a condition of sin-wrought slavery.

c) 2 Thessalonians 2:7–12

In the final outworking of disobedience, when all restraint is removed, the spirit of opposition to God must fully demonstrate itself. Then, we are here plainly warned, those who have 'refused to love the truth and so be saved' will become deceived followers of the only alternative, 'the lie', the devil's counterfeit. This God will deliberately allow for their judgment. Thus will their eternal condemnation as sinners be confirmed, because they 'not believed the truth but have delighted in wickedness'. So the only alternative to following the truth is believing the lie. (Cf. 1 John 1:6.)

d) Revelation 22:14,15

Those who read them will see that these words speak for themselves. They are among the last in the whole Bible.

They provide a brief, significant, final description of two types of character and of two corresponding destinies. 'They that do his commandments . . . have right to the tree of life, and may enter in through the gates into the city' (KJV). 'Outside are . . . everyone who loves and practises falsehood.' These are the only ultimate alternatives. It is between them that we all must make our choice.

2. The peril of disobedience

Disobedience is an ever-present danger, capable of involving us in eternal damage. All need to pay heed to the repeated witness and the solemn warnings of the Bible. It was by disobedience that the human race first fell into sin and came under God's condemnation (see Rom. 5:19a). It was because of disobedience that the people of Israel in Old Testament times repeatedly came under discipline and judgment. For instance, of the days of the Judges, we read

> The angel of the LORD went up from Gilgal to Bokim and said, "I brought you up out of Egypt and led you into the land that I swore to give to your forefathers. I said, 'I will never break my covenant with you, and you shall not make a covenant with the people of this land, but you shall break down their altars.' Yet you have disobeyed me. Why have you done this? Now therefore I tell you that I will not drive them out before you; they will be thorns in your sides and their gods will be a snare to you." (Judg. 2:1–3).

Similarly, in Samuel's day, we find the prophet solemnly warning the people

> If you fear the LORD and serve and obey him and do not rebel against his commands, and if both you and the king

who reigns over you follow the LORD your God—good! But if you do not obey the LORD, and if you rebel against his commands, his hand will be against you, as it was against your fathers. (1 Sam. 12:14,15).

Also, we find Samuel declaring to King Saul: 'Because you have rejected the word of the LORD, he has rejected you as king' (1 Sam. 15:23).

Later still, at the time of the separation of the kingdom of Israel from the kingdom of Judah, we learn that God said, 'See, I am going to tear the kingdom out of Solomon's hand . . . because they have forsaken me . . . and have not walked in my ways' (1 Kgs 11:31,33). Also, much later again, when even Jerusalem was destroyed, and the house of God burnt, and the people carried captive to Babylon, the writer summarizes the cause, by saying

The LORD, the God of their fathers, sent word to them through his messengers again and again, because he had pity on his people and on his dwelling place. But they mocked God's messengers, despised his words and scoffed at his prophets until the wrath of the LORD was aroused against his people and there was no remedy. He brought up against them the king of the Babylonians . . . God handed all of them over to Nebuchadnezzar. (2 Chr. 36:15–17)

When we turn to the New Testament we find that these happenings of Old Testament times are but 'figures of the true' and shadows and types of the final realities. There is now a greater Word from God, given to men and women in Christ, disobedience to which will involve us in eternal judgment.

We must pay more careful attention, therefore, to what we have heard, so that we do not drift away. For if the message

spoken by angels was binding, and every violation and disobedience received its just punishment, how shall we
escape if we ignore such a great salvation? This salvation,
which was first announced by the Lord, was confirmed to
us by those who heard him. (Heb. 2:1–3)

For the day is coming 'when the Lord Jesus is revealed
from heaven in blazing fire with his powerful angels'
and then He will act in judgment – 'punish those who do
not know God and do not obey the gospel of our Lord
Jesus. They will be punished with everlasting destruction and shut out from the presence of the Lord' (2 Thes.
1:7–9).

3. The crowning rewards of obedience

If disobedience to the Word of God must be followed by
inevitable judgment, the consequences of obedience to
God's Word are equally certain and surpassingly wonderful. Of these, the crowning reward is nothing less
than to become like to God, and therefore able to enjoy
fellowship with Him. It is, indeed, to realize 'the chief
end of man', which is 'to glorify God and to enjoy Him
for ever'.

a) John 14:15,21–24;15:14

Obedience to God's Word is first of all the proper and
only adequate sign of true love of God and of His Son,
Jesus Christ, our Lord. So our Saviour said explicitly and
repeatedly, 'If you love me, you will obey what I command.' 'Whoever has my commands and obeys them, he
is the one who loves me.' 'You are my friends if you do
what I command.' So the first reward of obedience to

His commandments is that, by it, we show our love to
Him who first loved us.

b) *John 14:21,23; 1 John 2:3,4; 3:24*

Such obedience to God's Word leads in the second place
to a significant consequence. Through it we are called to
enter into a deepening knowledge of God Himself, a
realized fellowship with the Father, through the Son,
and by the Spirit. So our Lord said of the one, who by
obedience to His commandments shows his or her love
to God, that 'He who loves me will be loved by my
Father, and I too will love him and show myself to him.'
And again, 'My Father will love him, and we will come
to him and make our home with him.'

Consequently, when in his first letter John deals with
the practical tests of vital Christian experience, he
writes: 'We know that we have come to know him if we
obey his commands. The man who says, "I know him,"
but does not do what he commands is a liar, and the
truth is not in him.' 'Those who obey his commands live
in him, and he in them.'

So the second reward of obedience to His commandments is that, through it, we come to know God in intimate personal communion: for only the obedient can
'enjoy Him for ever'.

c) *John 13:34; 15:12; 1 John 4:7,8,21*

Finally, obedience to God's Word must lead us to self-
forgetful and self-sacrificing love of others. For God
Himself is love of this kind. No one can respond to
God's Word, walk in God's ways, and live in God's company, without, as His child, beginning to reproduce the
family likeness; and that is love. So Jesus' new and

repeated command was, 'Love one another. As I have loved you, so you must love one another.' Or, as John puts it, 'And he has given us this command: Whoever loves God must also love his brother.' So the final reward of obedience to His commandments is that, by God's grace and through His Spirit, there should be expressed in us something of the very nature and character of God Himself: 'because God is love'.

ND - #0083 - 270225 - C0 - 198/129/15 - PB - 9781850788430 - Gloss Lamination